TOWARDS THE
NATIONAL CURRICULUM

7

TOWARDS THE NATIONAL CURRICULUM

Discussion and Control in the
English Educational System 1965-1988

W S Fowler

Books for Teachers

Series Editor: Tom Marjoram

First published in 1988 by
Kogan Page Ltd.
120 Pentonville Rd, London N1 9JN

Printed and bound in Great Britain by
Billing and Sons Ltd, Worcester

British Library Cataloguing in Publication Data

Fowler, W S
  Towards the national curriculum: discussion
  & control in the English educational system. –
  — (Kogan Page books for teachers).
  1. Great Britain. Secondary schools.
  Curriculum
  I. Title
  373.19'0941

ISBN 1 85091 580 6

CONTENTS

General Note

Schools Council publications, the work of the Assessment of Performance Unit and the build up to the new General Certificate of Secondary Education all contribute important elements in the development of curriculum thinking.

For reasons of space however, the present study confines itself to the part played in the process by Department of Education and Science and HM Inspectorate documents.

Extracts from official material are reproduced with the permission of the Controller of Her Majesty's Stationery Office. The author has used italics to emphasise various sections of the quoted extracts.

Chronology of Curriculum Discussions, Influences and Controls

INTRODUCTION

For the first hundred years of national education in England and Wales, the schools themselves were virtually 'on their own' in terms of ethos, organisation and curriculum. In practically no other country did individual institutions enjoy so much freedom, and in no other systems did the headteacher wield such absolute power.

Apart from some gentle touches on the tiller in the form of hortatory reports sponsored by the then Board of Education, this completely decentralised picture persisted. By the time of the swinging sixties the concept of free secondary education for all had been firmly established, the school leaving age was due to be raised to 16, and post-war building programmes had benefited from the expansionist mood of the era. And it was at this time that the first whiffs of educational innovation, central influence and control outlined here began to emerge.

The Secret Garden

The 1962 the 'forbidden question' in education was publicly posed by the now fully fledged educational arm of central government, namely the Ministry of Education. The Minister himself enquired about the content of the 'secret garden' of the curriculum. The key to this secret garden must be found and a method to unlock the garden must be discovered.

It was left to the Ministry's civil servants to forge the key. Their attempt at success took the form of a central group sited within the Ministry of Education itself, headed by a civil servant, and entitled the *Curriculum Study Group*.

However, this early notion of a governmental group concerning itself with school curricular matters provoked bitter hostility from the teaching profession and the local education authorities. Two years later the Curriculum Study Group was replaced by a national 'representative' body which was given the title of the *Schools Council*. This new council, funded jointly by central government and the local education authorities, was empowered to set up projects with two overall aims:

1. To assist schools to plan detailed curricular criteria;
2. To overhaul the examinations system which overshadowed all attempts at curricular reform and innovation.

By the end of the same year however, curricular intentions were destined to give way to a massive organisational change in the educational system introduced by a newly elected Labour government.

CHAPTER 1

THE INTRODUCTION OF COMPREHENSIVE EDUCATION (DES Circular 10/65)

The sea change in the education system in England and Wales upon which Harold Wilson's 1965 Government embarked was embodied in the proposal to replace the exiting 'tripartite' system of secondary schooling by a national comprehensive system.

The new system was to have the twin aims of:

1. Abolishing selection at the age of eleven plus;
2. Promoting national social cohesion by ensuring that all children of secondary age were educated together in the same type of school.

The instrument designed to achieve this national change was, perhaps surprisingly, not a new Education Act, but a simple administrative circular. This was despatched to all Local Education Authorities and the governing bodies of voluntary schools on 12 July 1965.

Listed as DES Circular 10/65 the circular is self explanatory and in view of its historic importance it is reproduced here in full:

Circular 10/65 – The Organisation of Secondary Education

I. Introduction

1. It is the Government's declared objective to end selection at eleven plus

and to eliminate separatism in secondary education. The Government's policy has been endorsed by the House of Commons in a motion passed on 21 January 1965:

> That this House, conscious of the need to raise educational standards at all levels, and regretting that the realisation of this objective is impeded by the separation of children into different types of secondary schools, notes with approval the efforts of local authorities to reorganise secondary education on comprehensive lines which will preserve all that is valuable in grammar school education for those children who now receive it and make it available to more children; recognises that the method and timing of such reorganisation should vary to meet local needs; and believes that the time is now ripe for a declaration of national policy.

The Secretary of State accordingly requests local education authorities, if they have not already done so, to prepare and submit to him plans for reorganising secondary education in their areas on comprehensive lines. The purpose of this Circular is to provide some central guidance on the methods by which this can be achieved.

II. Main forms of comprehensive organisation

2. There are a number of ways in which comprehensive education may be organised. While the essential needs of the children do not vary greatly from one area to another, the views of individual authorities, the distribution of population and the nature of existing schools will inevitably dictate different solutions in different areas. It is important that new schemes build on the foundation of present achievements and preserve what is best in existing schools.

3. Six main forms of comprehensive organisation have so far emerged from experience and discussion:

   (i) The orthodox comprehensive school with an age range of 11-18.
   (ii) A two-tier system whereby *all* pupils transfer at 11 to a junior comprehensive school and *all* go on at 13 or 14 to a senior comprehensive school.
   (iii) A two-tier system under which *all* pupils on leaving primary school transfer to a junior comprehensive school, but at the age of 13 or 14 *some* pupils move on to a senior school while *the remainder* stay on in the same school. There are two main variations: in one, the comprehensive school which all pupils enter after leaving primary school provides no course terminating in a public examination, and normally keeps pupils only until 15; in the other, this school provides G.C.E. and C.S.E. courses, keeps pupils at least until 16, and encourages transfer at the appropriate stage to the sixth form of the senior school.
   (iv) A two-tier system in which *all* pupils on leaving primary school transfer to a junior comprehensive school. At the age of 13 or 14 *all*

pupils have a choice between a senior school catering for those who expect to stay at school well beyond the compulsory age, and a senior school catering for those who do not.

(v) Comprehensive schools with an age range of 11 to 16 combined with sixth form colleges for pupils over 16.

(vi) A system of middle schools which straddle the primary/secondary age ranges. Under this system pupils transfer from a primary school at the age of 8 or 9 to a comprehensive school with an age range of 8 to 12 or 9 to 13. From this middle school they move on to a comprehensive school with an age range of 12 or 13 to 18.

4. The most appropriate system will depend on local circumstances and an authority may well decide to adopt more than one form of organisation in the area for which it is responsible. Organisations of types (i), (ii), (v) and (vi) produce schools which are fully comprehensive in character. On the other hand an organisation of type (iii) or (iv) is not fully comprehensive in that it involves the separation of children of differing aims and aptitudes into different schools at the age of 13 or 14. Given the limitations imposed by existing buildings such schemes are acceptable as interim solutions, since they secure many of the advantages of comprehensive education and in some areas offer the most satisfactory method of bringing about reorganisation at an early date. But they should be regarded only as an interim stage in development towards a fully comprehensive secondary organisation.

5. Against this general background, the Secretary of State wishes to make certain comments on each of the system described in paragraph 3:

(i) Orthodox comprehensive schools 11 to 18 (see paragraph 3(i))

6. There is now a considerable volume of experience of all-through comprehensive schools; and it is clear that they can provide an effective and educationally sound secondary organisation. If it were possible to design a new pattern of secondary education without regard to existing buildings, the all-through comprehensive school would in many respects provide the simplest and best solution. There are therefore strong arguments for its adoption wherever circumstances permit.

7. In practice, however, circumstances will usually not permit, since the great majority of post-war schools and of those now being built are designed as separate secondary schools and are too small to be used as all-through comprehensive schools. There is, of course, some scope for building new schools of this type; and it should be borne in mind that such schools need not be as large as was once thought necessary to produce a sixth form of economic size. It is now clear that a six or seven form entry school can cater properly for the whole ability range and produce a viable sixth form. In rural areas or in small towns where only one secondary school is needed, its size will inevitably be determined by the number of children for whom it must cater; and this may well not support a six form

entry school. But wherever a six form entry is possible, within the limits of reasonable travelling for secondary pupils, it should be achieved.

8. It will sometimes be possible to establish a single comprehensive in buildings designed for use as separate schools. But any scheme of this type will need careful scrutiny. If buildings are at a considerable distance from each other, or separated by busy roads, the disadvantages are obvious. Even where they are close together the amount and type of accommodation available may cause groupings of pupils which are arbitrary and educationally inefficient. It is essential 'that any such school could make a satisfactory timetable, deploy its staff efficiently, economically and without undue strain, and become a well-knit community.

9. There are examples of schools which function well in separate buildings and there will often be advantages to offset the disadvantages mentioned above. For example, the sharing of different premises by a single school may ensure that all the children enjoy at least part of their secondary education in a new building. Moreover additional building already approved or likely to be included in an early programme may help to overcome the drawbacks of the initial arrangements.

(ii) Two-tier systems whereby all pupils transfer at 11 to a junior comprehensive school and at 13 or 14 to a senior comprehensive school (see paragraph 3(ii))

10. Two-tier systems consisting of junior and senior comprehensive schools, each with its own head teacher, and with automatic transfer of all pupils at 13 or 14, have two clear advantages over other two-tier systems. They avoid discrimination between pupils at the point of transfer; and they eliminate the element of guesswork about the proportion of pupils who will transfer to the senior school. They may, it is true, produce problems of organisation, particularly where a senior school is fed by more than one junior school. If pupils are not to suffer unnecessarily from the change of school, the schools involved will have to co-operate fully and positively in the choice of curriculum, syllabus and teaching method (see paragraph 34). In the interest of continuity all the schools will have to surrender some of their freedom. But this system is attractive in that it will often fit readily into existing buildings; and it can develop into an all-through system of orthodox comprehensive schools in the course of time as new buildings become available.

(iii) A two-tier system under which all pupils transfer at 11 to a junior comprehensive school and at 13 or 14 some pupils move on to a senior school while others remain in the junior school (see paragraph 3(iii))

11. The two main forms which this system may take have been described in paragraph 3(iii) above. That in which the junior comprehensive school keeps pupils only until 15 can clearly be no more than an interim arrangement; there must eventually be automatic transfer of all pupils from the junior to the senior school.

12. If local circumstances rule this out for some years then at the very least there should be a reorganisation of the junior schools to make satisfactory provision until 16 for those pupils who do not transfer at 13 or 14. Such provision will certainly have to include courses leading to the C.S.E. examination; whether it should also include G.C.E. Ordinary level courses is a more open question. Where staffing permits, there is much to be said for including G.C.E. courses in the junior schools. This gives an added stimulus to the work and to the teaching; it gives intellectually able pupils who do not transfer an opportunity nevertheless of gaining the qualifications which they would have won if they had transferred; it makes it easier for them, through gaining G.C.E. Ordinary levels, to transfer in due course to the sixth form in a senior school or to a college for further education; and it reduces the danger of creating social differences between junior and senior schools, with the junior schools regarded as 'poor relations'.

13. Whatever dividing line is drawn between the junior and the senior school, the Secretary of State will expect certain conditions to be observed:

(a) It is essential, if selection is not to be reintroduced, that transfer to the senior school should be at parents' choice.
(b) Guidance to parents on transfer should be given on an organised basis and should not take the form of advice by one teacher only.
(c) Guidance should ensure that children who would benefit from a longer or more intellectual course are not deprived of it by reason simply of their parents' lack of knowledge of what is involved. The parents must have the final decision; but parents from less educated homes in particular should have a full explanation of the opportunities open to their children.
(d) The junior school must be staffed and its curriculum devised so as to cater effectively for the whole ability range in the first two or three years. This is of great importance whatever transfer age is chosen; but with a transfer age of 14 it becomes critical. The more able children must not be held back or denied the range of subjects and quality of teaching which they would have enjoyed in a grammar school. Equally, their needs must not be met at the expense of other children.

14. If these conditions are met schemes of this type have the merit of fitting comparatively easily into existing buildings and of taking full account of parental choice at the point of transfer. They are therefore acceptable as transitional schemes. But eventually, as paragraphs 4 and 11 will have made clear, the Secretary of State expects that all two-tier systems involving optional transfer at 13 or 14 will give way to systems under which transfer is automatic.

(iv) Two-tier systems whereby all pupils transfer at 11 to a junior comprehensive school with a choice of senior school at 13 or 14 (see paragraph 3(iv))

15. These differ from the schemes described in paragraphs 11 to 14 in that the junior comprehensive school has the same age range for all its pupils. No children remain in it beyond the age of 13 or 14. All pupils then have a choice of senior school; one senior school will aim at Advanced level and other sixth form work, while the other will not take its pupils beyond Ordinary level, although the dividing line between the schools can be drawn at different points and they may overlap. The comments made in paragraphs 12, 13 and 14 above apply equally to schemes of this kind.

(v) Comprehensive schools with an age range of 11 to 16 combined with a sixth form college for pupils of 16 and over (see paragraph 3(v))

16. Two conceptions of the sixth form college have been put forward. One envisages the establishment of colleges catering for the educational needs of all young people staying on at school beyond the age of 16; the other would make entry to a college dependent on the satisfaction of certain conditions (eg five passes at Ordinary level or a declared intention of preparing for Advanced level). A variation of the sixth form college pattern is that which attaches the sixth form unit to one school; under such an arrangement pupils from schools without sixth forms can transfer to a single sixth form at another school.

17. A sixth form college may involve disadvantages for the lower schools; there are few obvious arguments in favour of comprehensive schools with an age range of 11 to 16. Children in this age group may lose from a lack of contact with senior pupils of 16 to 18. There is a danger that the concentration of scarce specialist teachers in the sixth form college will drain too much talent away from the schools. Some teachers may find unattractive the prospect of teaching the whole ability range in a school offering no opportunities for advanced work and many teachers express a preference for work in schools catering for the whole secondary age range.

18. But the possibility of loss to the lower schools has to be weighed against possible gains to pupils in the sixth form colleges. The risk of draining away teaching talent from the lower schools may be outweighed by the concentration of specialist staff in the colleges, thus ensuring their more economic use; a point of particular importance while the present teacher shortages continue. The loss to the younger pupils from lack of contact with sixth forms may be outweighed, not only by the greater opportunities for leadership which the younger pupils themselves will have in the lower school, but also by the gain to the sixth formers from their attaining something of the status and freedom from traditional school discipline enjoyed by students.

19. It is essential that no scheme involving the establishment of a sixth form college should lead to any restriction of existing educational opportunities for young people of 16 to 18. Where authorities are considering the establishment of sixth form colleges they should review all the educational needs of the 16-18 group in their area and the provision they

have hitherto made for them, both in sixth forms and in colleges of further education. Where, in the light of this review, it is proposed to establish sixth form colleges, the relationship between these colleges and colleges of further education, and their respective functions, will require careful consideration to avoid unnecessary duplication of resources and to ensure that the best use is made of the educational potential of each.

20. In this country there is so far little experience on which to base final judgements on the merits of sixth form colleges. Nevertheless the Secretary of State believes that the issues have been sufficiently debated to justify a limited number of experiments. Where authorities contemplate the submission of proposals, he hopes that they will consult with his Department at an early stage.

(vi) An organisation which involves middle schools straddling the primary/secondary age ranges (see paragraph 3(vi))

21. Section 1 of the Education Act 1964 makes it legally possible for new schools to be established which cater for an age range covering both primary and secondary schools as defined in Section 8 of the Education Act 1944. The establishment of middle schools with age ranges of 8 to 12 or 9 to 13 has an immediate attraction in the context of secondary reorganisation on comprehensive lines. In the first place such schools seem to lead naturally to the elimination of selection. In the second they shorten the secondary school span by one or two years and thus make it possible to have smaller all-through comprehensive schools.

22. Notwithstanding the *prima facie* attractiveness of middle school systems the Secretary of State does not intend to give his statutory approval to more than a very small number of such proposals in the near future. This is for reasons relating to the age of transfer from primary to secondary education; see paragraph 30 below.

III. Some general considerations

(i) Buildings

23. The disposition, character and size of existing schools, particularly of the schools built since the war which must be assumed to remain in use for a considerable time, must influence and in many cases go far to determine the shape of secondary organisation. Sometimes the existing buildings will lend themselves readily to a new organisation; in other cases they will exhibit marked deficiencies if they are used, with little or no modification, for purposes for which they were not intended.

24. During the next few years growing demands for new schools arising from the increase in the school population, new house building and the raising of the school leaving age are unlikely to permit any relaxation of the criteria for inclusion of projects in building programmes. It would not be realistic for authorities to plan on the basis that their individual

programmes will be increased solely to take account of the need to adapt or remodel existing buildings on a scale which would not have been necessary but for reorganisation.

25. Where existing buildings cannot easily be adapted to a new pattern authorities, in drawing up their plans, must balance against each other the following factors:

(a) the consideration mentioned in paragraph 24:
(b) the educational disadvantages which may attach to schemes designed to make use of existing buildings where these do not lend themselves adequately to a comprehensive system:
(c) the possibility of recasting building programmes announced but not yet implemented (see paragraph 44(b) below).

26. It is for authorities to weigh these considerations and to devise the most satisfactory plans in relation to local circumstances. In doing so, they should appreciate that while the Secretary of State wishes progress to be as rapid as possible, he does not wish it to be achieved by the adoption of plans whose educational disadvantages more than off-set the benefits which will flow from the adoption of comprehensive schooling.

(ii) Staffing

27. The changeover to a comprehensive system should not affect the numerical demand for teachers significantly. But the short-term plan called for in paragraph 44(b) will have to be devised against the background that the secondary schools will still be short of teachers in 1969 (though their staffing standards will be better then than now) and have still to face the staffing strain of a higher leaving age in 1970–71. The Secretary of State will not be able to modify the quota arrangements to take account of individual authorities' proposals in response to this Circular.

28. It will be clear from Section II above that reorganisation can have other important and complex implications for staffing; see, for example, the comments on staffing in particular types of scheme contained in paragraphs 13(d) and 17. Authorities should consider carefully how best to effect any redistribution of teaching staff which their plans may entail and, in particular, how to ensure that specialist staff in scarce categories are deployed and used as efficiently as possible.

29. Plans to reorganise secondary education are bound to affect the pattern of higher posts in the schools, especially headships. The Secretary of State is glad to note that the Burnham Primary and Secondary Committee has under consideration the question of safeguarding teachers' salaries in the event of school reorganisation.

(iii) Age of transfer to secondary education

30. Pending any recommendations which the English and Welsh Central

Advisory Councils for Education might make on the age of transfer from primary to secondary education, the normal age of transfer should be regarded as eleven plus. Except where they have agreed a limited departure from this principle with the Secretary of State, authorities should prepare their plans on this basis. Decisions taken by the Secretary of State when he considers the Councils' recommendations may have a bearing on secondary school organisation but this situation is not likely to arise in the near future. Authorities will appreciate that there is bound to be a considerable period between the making of any recommendations and the implementation of Government decisions on them; these would be reached only after wide consultation and careful consideration of all the factors involved.

(iv) Transfer from junior to senior secondary schools in two-tier systems

31. With a school leaving age of 16, authorities adopting a two-tier organisation, including organisations of the type described in paragraph 3(iii), will have a choice between a three-year course in the junior secondary school and a two-year course subsequently, or vice versa. Two years is not ideal as a period in one school at any stage; but a choice has to be made, and the balance of argument seems to favour transfer to a senior school at 13.

32. If the age of transfer were 14, pupils would enter the senior school at a stage when the number of subjects studied was being reduced and the course began to focus more narrowly on examinations. Some subjects would never be begun, either because they needed a course of some years or because they were not subjects which the particular pupil needed to offer in an examination. Although for subjects such as history and geography the age chosen for transfer might not be very important, for others, such as science and modern languages, delay of transfer until 14 would probably be harmful. A two-year course geared to an external examination would be likely to be planned on the basis of giving a large amount of time to comparatively few subjects; this is the very reverse of liberal education.

33. With 13 as the age of transfer the senior school could afford to introduce specialisation more gradually, and there would be more likelihood of effecting a smooth transition. Arguments in favour of a three-year run in the junior school apply with even greater force to the senior school, where the pace is accelerated and the course reaches its climax both for pupils who have to face examinations and for those about to enter the world of work.

34. A change of school is a stimulus for some pupils but for others it means a loss of momentum; the break imposed by transfer therefore calls for a deliberate effort to bridge it. To achieve continuity close co-operation between the staff of the different schools will be necessary, particularly where several junior schools feed one senior school, in the choice of

curriculum, syllabus and teaching method. If a two-tier system is to function efficiently, there will also be a need for systematic and continuous guidance and observation of pupils' development, together with careful recording of findings and a regular exchange of information and views between junior and senior schools.

35. In two-tier systems which allow a choice of school during the secondary course (see the forms of organisation described under subheading II (iii) and (iv) above), it is important to ensure that children whose parents choose the lower school for them when they are 13 or 14 should be able to transfer to the senior school at the sixth form stage as a matter of right, if by this stage they find that they wish to continue in full-time education at school. But, as has already been made clear, the Secretary of State expects that optional will eventually give way to automatic transfer.

(v) The school community

36. A comprehensive school aims to establish a school community in which pupils over the whole ability range and with differing interests and backgrounds can be encouraged to mix with each other, gaining stimulus from the contacts and learning tolerance and understanding in the process. But particular comprehensive schools will reflect the characteristics of the neighbourhood in which they are situated. If their community is less varied and fewer of the pupils come from homes which encourage educational interests, schools may lack the stimulus and vitality which schools in other areas enjoy. The Secretary of State therefore urges authorities to ensure, when determining catchment areas, that schools are as socially and intellectually comprehensive as is practicable. In a two-tier system it may be possible to link two differing districts so that all pupils from both areas go to the same junior and then to the same senior comprehensive schools.

(vi) Voluntary schools

37. In a number of areas which have already introduced or planned a comprehensive organisation the voluntary schools have not been included, but the plans which the Secretary of State is now requesting authorities to prepare should embrace them. Authorities which have already devised their plans for county (and sometimes controlled) schools alone should take the initiative in opening discussions with the governors of the aided and special agreement schools which they maintain and where appropriate, with diocesan authorities, with a view to reaching agreement on how these schools can best be reorganised on comprehensive lines. Other authorities should proceed with consultation and planning for voluntary schools as part of their general planning. It will clearly be of great assistance, particularly in areas with a large number of voluntary school places, if negotiations can lead to the early integration of voluntary schools into a reorganised structure. The Secretary of State asks that local education authorities and the governors of voluntary schools should enter into discussions to this end at the earliest practicable stage in the preparation of plans.

38. It is not essential that the same pattern should be adopted for denominational and other voluntary schools in any given area as is adopted for that area's county schools. The disposition and nature of the existing voluntary school buildings may dictate a different solution; voluntary schools of a particular denomination may serve the population of more than one local authority area, and the school or diocesan authorities may be able to devise an appropriate and acceptable scheme which does not coincide directly with that adopted for the authorities' county schools: or a denomination may at present rely heavily on direct grant schools for its selective places. There will not be a single and easy solution to these difficulties, but the Secretary of State hopes that where they occur, the schools, denominational authorities and local education authorities will be able to negotiate solutions which ensure that while selection is eliminated, parents are not deprived of places which meet their religious wishes, and on which they have hitherto been able to rely.

(vii) Direct grant schools

39. In a number of areas, and especially in large towns, direct grant grammar schools make a substantial contribution alongside the maintained schools to the provision of secondary places. The proportion of such places paid for by local education authorities is in the case of many schools, particularly those of a denominational character, very high. The Secretary of State looks to both local education authorities and the governors of direct grant schools to consider ways of maintaining and developing this co-operation in the context of the new policy of comprehensive education. He hopes that authorities will study ways in which the schools might be associated with their plans, and that governing bodies will be ready to consider changes, for instance in curriculum and in method and age of entry, which will enable them to participate fully in the local scheme. The Secretary of State asks that authorities should open discussions at an early stage with the governors of direct grant schools in which they take up places; it may be appropriate for such discussions to be in consultation with any other authorities taking up places in the same schools.

(viii) Consultation

40. The smooth inception and continuing success of any scheme of reorganisation will depend on the co-operation of teachers and the support and confidence of parents. To secure these there must be a process of consultation and explanation before any scheme is approved by an authority for submission to the Secretary of State. An authority should take all those concerned into its confidence at as early a stage as possible.

41. The proper processes of local government must leave initiative on matters of principle and the ultimate responsibility for decisions with the elected representatives of the community. But the Secretary of State believes that once the principles and main outlines of a possible plan of reorganisation have been formulated there should follow a period of close

and genuine consultation with teachers. The precise methods cannot be prescribed and will necessarily vary from one authority to another. On the general character of a plan and on matters affecting an authority's teachers as a whole consultation with teachers' associations would normally be appropriate. Working groups composed of local education authority officers and teachers have also been found successful in some areas. Individual teachers or school staffs affected by particular schemes should always be taken into consultation, to whatever extent is reasonable and practicable, at the appropriate stage. The arrangements must strike a balance between the fundamental right and duty of the authority to take decisions and the practical good sense of accepting that teachers have a very real contribution to make from their knowledge of the children and their needs. In the last resort only teachers can make any educational system work well.

42. Parents cannot be consulted in the same way as teachers; but it is important that they should be informed fully and authoritatively as soon as practicable in the planning stage. Explanations by elected members and officers can be given at meetings, in schools, in booklets and through the press. A scheme may easily arouse anxiety and hostility among parents if they are dependent for information about it on unreliable and incomplete reports spread by word of mouth or partisan reports of any kind. The early and widespread dissemination of information will help to strengthen parental confidence and should avoid the risk of the submission of ill-informed and unnecessary objections where schemes involve the publication of notices under Section 13 of the 1944 Act.

IV. Preparation and submission of plans

43. In the light of the considerations mentioned above, local education authorities are requested to submit plans to the Secretary of State for the reorganisation of secondary education in their areas on comprehensive lines.

44. Plans should be submitted within one year of the date of this Circular, although the Secretary of State may exceptionally agree an extension to this period in the case of any individual authority. Plans should be in two parts (15 copies of each) as follows:

(a) *A general statement of the authority's long-term proposals*
    This should indicate the type or types of comprehensive organisation which it is intended to establish; should cover all parts of the authority's area: and should embrace in its scope both county and voluntary maintained schools. It will be clear from paragraphs 37 and 38 above that voluntary schools should in due course be as fully part of any scheme as county schools, though they need not follow an identical pattern and it may take longer for the necessary adjustments to be achieved. Authorities which at present supplement their

maintained provision by taking free or reserved places in direct grant schools or by paying fees in whole or in part for pupils at independent schools should indicate their future intentions. They should also indicate the extent to which direct grant schools are participating in their plans.

(b) *A detailed statement of the authority's proposals, whether or not they have already been discussed with the Department, covering a period of three years starting not later than September 1967*

This part should describe what it is proposed by the authority should happen to every secondary school affected by this first stage of their plan. It should be made clear whether what is proposed for this period is an instalment of a long-term plan or whether it represents interim arrangements designed to be modified or superseded. Each school affected should be identified by name, present size, status, denomination, sex of pupils and type. Its short- and long-term future should then be described.

The arrangements proposed for the admission of children to the comprehensive schools should be explained. This explanation should cover initial admission to schools recruiting at the normal age of transfer from primary to secondary education and any later transfer which is involved in two-tier systems.

This three-year instalment of the plan should include a statement of estimates of costs of all major and minor building programme proposals which will be involved in carrying it out. The Secretary of State does not intend to amend of his own initiative the major school building programmes already announced for 1965–66, 1966–67 and part of 1967–68. But authorities may themselves wish to recast some of their programmes in order to bring secondary school projects into line with their plans for reorganisation; in this case proposals for recasting programmes should be made at the time of the plan's submission. When preparing such proposals authorities will need to bear in mind the building needs created in their areas by the raising of the school leaving age in 1970–71. The total cost of a recast programme must not exceed that already authorised for 1965–66 and 1966–67; there may however be some scope for increase in 1967–68 since the full programme for that year has not yet been settled.

45. The Secretary of State hopes that local education authorities, voluntary school governors, denominational representatives and direct grant school governors will consult freely with the officers of his Department at any stage in their deliberations at which they believe that informal discussion would be helpful. He would in particular ask that local education authorities should consult the Department when their plans are at a sufficiently advanced stage but before they are finally approved for submission.

46. The Government are aware that the complete elimination of selection and separatism in secondary education will take time to achieve. They do not seek to impose destructive or precipitate change on existing schools;

they recognise that the evolution of separate schools into a comprehensive system must be a constructive process requiring careful planning by local education authorities in consultation with all those concerned. But the spontaneous and exciting progress which has been made in this direction by so many authorities in recent years demonstrates that the objective is not only practicable; it is also now widely accepted. The Govenment believe that both the education service and the general public will welcome the further impetus which a clear statement of national policy will secure.

AFTERMATH OF THE CIRCULAR

Following the issue of Circular 10/65, the reorganisation of secondary education on comprehensive lines in England and Wales proceeded at a fitful but accelerating pace with the result that a decade later 70 per cent of all secondary school children were being educated in some form of comprehensive system. By the 1980s this figure had risen to 90 per cent.

Ages of transfer to secondary schooling

An important byproduct of the circular was the occurrence of widespread change in the age of transfer from primary to secondary education. The hitherto generally accepted age of eleven plus was superseded up and down the country by reorganisation schemes which entailed transfer age at virtually any age after seven.

The proposals outlined in the circular encouraged, very often for administrative and financial reasons, schemes whereby 'first schools' catering for age range of 5–8 years were established. Transfer at eight was to an 8–12 'middle' school, to be followed by a 12–16 or a 12–18 secondary school. Other LEAs adopted a 5–9 first school pattern with transfer to the middle school for the 9–13 age range, followed by a 13–18 age grouping for the secondary level. A number of authorities retained the secondary transfer age at 11, but instigated a further change at the age of 14 plus. In some areas all pupils transferred schools at this age while in others only the more academic pupils moved on to a new school.

In addition to the 'traditional' comprehensive idea of large all-through 11–18 schools, some local authorities instituted a system of sixth-form colleges whereby all pupils enjoyed a secondary span of 11–16 years, followed by open access or selective access to a sixth-form college.

In a further variant of comprehensivisation further education colleges became the 'top tier' of secondary education under an all embracing 'tertiary college' concept.

Thus as the theory of comprehensivisation turned into practice on a national scale, social and educational ideals were to become enmeshed in an administrative and parental confusion of illogical variety.

CHAPTER 2

THE EXPANSION OF EDUCATION

Education: A Framework for Expansion

Following the election of a Conservative Government in 1970, the Ministry of Education (by now rechristened the Department of Education and Science and led by Margaret Thatcher) proposed the framework for a number of major initiatives involving a considerable increase in capital expenditure on the educational system.

These proposals became public in December 1972, in the form of a White Paper entitled *Education: A Framework for Expansion*. The White Paper devoted a major part of its intentions to the further and higher education spheres. Its proposals for primary and secondary schools were succinctly summarised thus:

Primary and secondary schools (including nursery schools and classes for the under-fives) still claim more than half the total of educational expenditure, in spite of the rapid growth of higher education over the past decade. Resources apart, the schools are of paramount importance because they provide the foundation for all continued education, and because they affect almost the whole population of the country at some stage in their lives. In 1971 over 93 per cent of all the children of compulsory school age in England and Wales were attending maintained primary or secondary schools.

The Government have carried through to finality a great reform, the raising of the school leaving age to 16 in accordance with the provisions of the Education Act, 1944. They have also devoted substantial additional resources to the replacement and improvement of unsatisfactory primary schools. The next phase of the Government's policy for the schools, which is set out in the following sections of this White Paper, makes advances which are no less important. These include a major initiative in the provision of facilities for the under-fives. In addition to this important extension of the range of education, plans have been made for increased capital expenditure on the improvement of secondary schools and on an enlarged special school building programme; and for a ten-year programme for improving school staffing standards and the extension to all teachers of opportunities for in-service training.

No mention of the school curriculum itself is made in this White Paper and it is worth noting that, as recently as 1972, central government appeared content to address itself to the provision of improved material conditions under which the schools themselves might plan and operate.

CHAPTER 3

GOOD SCHOOLS

The contribution of HM Inspectorate

It was thus left to HM Inspectors of Schools, acting independently, to begin asking some fundamental questions, and indeed perhaps one of the most fundamental of all educational questions: 'What makes a good school good?'

TEN GOOD SCHOOLS

Having set itself this question in 1975, the inspectorate attempted to answer it in a discussion paper entitled *Ten Good Schools*. The modus operandi of the enquiry was described in the introduction to the paper:

The object of this exercise, then, was to look at some aspects of a few secondary schools deemed to be 'successful'; first, to identify characteristics that might be emulated in any school and, secondly, to consider how far such characteristics constitute a common ground of values and objectives shared by schools that differ widely in circumstance. Limits of time and manpower precluded any attempt at comprehensive assessment, and the outcome was in any case intended to be impressionistic and subjective, offering material for discussion. However, to ensure some consistency of approach, visiting panels were asked to give attention to seven aspects in each of the schools. These were:

1. Fundamental objectives, and their realisation in relationships, discipline, curricular policies and the personal and social development of the pupils;

2. Pastoral care and oversight of academic progress, including administration, organisation, communications and the definition of roles and responsibility for staff and pupils;

3. Curriculum design and organisation (especially appropriateness to the developing needs and capacities of the pupils), content, choice and

balance, and planning and coordination and critical interest in new ideas as the part of the staff;

4. Staffing and quality of work, including clarity of intention and presentation, levels of expectation and standards of response;

5. Use of premises and resources, particularly the degree to which the quality of life of the school and the distinctive characteristics of its work are reflected in the environment it creates;

6. Links with the local community, including contacts with parents, interaction with the community outside school, and co-operation with other local services;

7. Leadership and 'climate'.

Each aspect of the profile of a good school which the enquiry covered is worthy of careful attention and evaluation. For present curricular purposes however, it will suffice to reproduce the fourth section of the findings.

Curriculum design and academic organisation

As far as content is concerned, there is general agreement that, for the years of compulsory schooling, the humanities, mathematics, science, creative arts, physical and spiritual development should be the elements common to all curricula. There is general agreement, too, that within this framework there should be opportunities in the latter part of the course for options which will match career interests, preferences and the emerging abilities of the individual, provided that a degree of specialisation that would prevent choice of advanced course or career is avoided. Examination requirements are accepted as a legitimate goal at this stage, provided that they do not dominate the programme, distort the balance of the curriculum or set unrealistic targets for the student. It is commonly held that able pupils as they grow older require opportunities to study in depth, to embrace the ideals of scholarship and to become increasingly responsible for their own habits of study and their own progress. Most would declare their belief in the continuing need, at this stage, for opportunities in practical and aesthetic pursuits and for general studies: that is, for the discussion and study of broad philosophical, social and cultural questions that may not fall within the purview of an examination.

Such criteria are satisfied in the schools under review, although their solutions to the problems differ. All have given considerable time and thought to the problems of academic organisation and curriculum design. In the larger schools policy is often determined by an academic board or a curriculum committee and implemented through a departmental or faculty structure. Some had set up working parties to review organisation: in the direct grant school, for example, a small working party had marshalled all the departmental arguments in favour of a five-year course for all in preference to the existing system which promoted able boys to the sixth form after four years.

None of the schools seeks to solve the problem of matching the curriculum to ability by fine streaming, though setting in certain subjects is common. The unit of organisation in the first one, two or three years in about half the schools is the mixed ability form; in the rest, pupils are divided by ability into three broad bands. One or two schools use both patterns at different stages. In those schools which for social and educational reasons have deliberately chosen to adopt mixed ability grouping there is critical awareness of the difficulties involved. The problem is how to individualise the teaching in ways which keep pupils at full stretch and yet provide a common starting point for all and equal opportunity to contribute to a common outcome. Much effort has been put into elaborating work sheets which take account of variations in reading ability and of general competence. Some teachers now find that this is tipping the balance towards individual work unduly and that pupils are being denied the stimulation and help that class discussion and teaching can bring, and experiment to achieve the right balance continues.

All the non-selective schools experiment with different kinds of organisation and different teaching methods for slow learners; they are constantly assessing the effects of their experiments. It is recognised that remedial departments have the disadvantage of removing the less able from the company of their contemporaries for too much of the week even though the work of the remedial class can be more easily integrated and designed to meet their needs exclusively. On the other hand a system of withdrawing the less able from normal classes, while it can help to remedy specific weaknesses of backward children, can provide too little support for the dull or severely retarded who on return to their normal class tend to flounder. Once again, the search is for a proper balance in provision.

Some schools superimpose on their form organisation a grouping into lower, middle and upper schools so as to create more homogeneous age groups with which the pupils can identify and within which broad educational aims can be seen and followed more obviously. The school in split premises has endeavoured to turn the division to advantage by giving the lower section a senior master and mistress of its own and a freedom to develop its own ethos and ways of working.

In general, the first three years have a common curriculum and all the schools ensure that creative subjects are given a fair proportion of time throughout. One comprehensive school in a poor area is well satisfied with its traditional organisation and curriculum. The common course comprises the traditional subjects, there is no experiment in integrated studies, and innovations such as computer studies and control technology are left to a later stage. The policy of the headmaster is to make haste slowly in order to carry parents, pupils and staff along at a pace they can tolerate. He would like to experiment with combined studies and with new patterns of teacher co-operation because he believes that the curriculum might gain in meaning and richness and the teaching in variety and quality. But by innovating judiciously, he tempers idealism and ambition with realism and common sense: the curriculum suits the pupils because it matches their expectations. The junior high school also sees its function in terms of building sound foundations through a common curriculum for all its pupils: "The high school's function is to provide a broad, general, liberalising education which will serve as a foundation for the more specialised work in the upper school. We have accordingly tried to meet our pupils' learning potential by a challenging curriculum, embracing a full range of subjects, with a time allocation common to all three years."

But innovation is not lacking and has been greatly facilitated by the importance attached to regular departmental consultation. In many of the schools in the sample departmental or faculty meetings are timetabled weekly. Some schools have set up working parties on curriculum development; others have encouraged innovation within subject areas by block time-tabling. This appears to be having a beneficial effect on learning and teaching since the choice of activity and the time given to it are more easily varied and the grouping of pupils and staff is more flexible. A large comprehensive school has adopted a faculty rather than a subject structure and the curriculum is conceived in terms of five broad areas: science and mathematics, English and modern languages; creative studies, social studies, and religious education; physical education; and careers education. Some of the schools are also experimenting with integrated studies: humanities courses which embrace English, history, geography and religious studies are common. In one school the course in humanities is a common course taken by all fourth formers. It is not only good in itself but, introduced at this stage for all pupils, it has been found to have a valuable unifying effect on the school. Other integrated courses encountered included environmental science (a first year course in science and geography) and the making of the landscape (a fourth and fifth year course in history and geography). A very interesting and successful example of an integrated course is outdoor education, a course for second-year pupils at the direct grant school which is a hybrid of environmental studies and outdoor physical training. Joint planning with a university department of education means that four university staff and 12 postgraduate students are available to assist the school staff. Six groups of ten pupils have each the help of two university students and a member of staff. One half day a week is given to field study and the aim of the course is to discover by personal observation what use man has made of the local river valley from its source to its mouth. The disciplines brought to bear include mathematics, physics, chemistry and biology, history, geography, geology and English. School syllabuses in these subjects are adapted to take account of and prepare for the possibilities of field work. Each week the pupils produce written work arising from the topic and at the end of the year submit an individual project. In the field, pupils receive training in orienteering, canoeing, pony trekking, walking and camping. The scheme has proved so successful that its extension to the third year is under consideration.

Another example of the way in which traditional subjects can be made more exciting to youngsters is the technical activities course in the independent school included in the sample. A beginning is made in the third year as part of the timetabled, rotational course in practical activities; thereafter it flourishes as a voluntary club activity. The aim is to encourage the pupils to identify their need for knowledge and skill arising from a technological project, to investigate and study their problems, to apply what they learn to the construction of their model and then to evaluate their results. Beginning with simple tasks of building a power-controlled model boat or aircraft, the boys later design their own projects such as radio-controlled model vehicles, ships and aircraft, a self-controlling solar heating dish, a hovercraft, tracked vehicles and electronic timing devices for photography. Some 48 different projects were under construction at the time of the visit to the school and much of the work seen was of outstanding ingenuity and quality. The scheme patently develops a high degree of creative ability and an attitude of enquiry and investigation; it amply fulfils the school's broad aim of 'encouraging self-expression and self-realisation through creative activity'.

An unusual example of integrated studies is the course at the same school which is labelled 'predicament, experiment and belief' and which extends through the first three years. Its object is to present to younger boys an integrated view of man in his physical environment in the past and present and of the religious beliefs whereby he gives meaning to his experience. The emphasis is on understanding the techniques of study in the disciplines involved rather than on amassing factual knowledge. The course has been in operation for nine years and is constantly revised. The staff involved meet for planning sessions weekly and they have built up a considerable range of resources, including books to support the work. The interests of the pupils is lively, the approach is scholarly and the work produced has significance and quality.

Curriculum choice at the fourth year stage is, as in most schools, a common feature. What is particularly interesting is the width of choice offered and the careful planning and guidance that ensures that a pupil's curriculum remains coherent and balanced. Schools without a generous staffing ratio managed to offer choices from combinations of subjects in such a way that other sections of the school were not unduly robbed of man-power. Planning is also imaginative for the less able or less well-motivated pupil. The modern school with 1,350 pupils on roll, for example, offers a guided choice of five subjects from five combinations totalling 60 courses which are added to the common core of religious education, English, mathematics, physical education and citizenship. Everyone has to take science but the course may be general science, physical science, biology, chemistry or human biology. New subjects such as community work projects, motor vehicle engineering or parentcraft are introduced to tempt the less academically interested to renewed effort. The large comprehensive school which regards its policy as a traditional one places pupils at this stage in three bands: those taking

GCE or CSE examinations in a choice of 20 subjects; those taking CSE only, with 19 subjects offered, and, for the less able, an integrated course. The last provides a choice of 13 subjects and includes studies such as computer science, and home-making together with a common core of English, mathematics, social studies and science all linked in the study of common themes such as 'war and society'. Health, careers and physical education are compulsory and taught separately to these pupils.

The problem of providing for the less able or the poorly motivated is acute for the large 13 to 18 school in a depressed area in northern England. An outward-looking course is being developed, called the 'school-based course', which has no set syllabus but involves local visits and work experience followed by a variety of work in school, arising from what the pupils have seen and done. Originally it was designed for one day a week, but its success is such that next year it will operate on every day of the week. In addition, the school has made special arrangements for the small group of pupils whose learning and behavioural problems have proved exceptionally difficult to cope with in the normal classroom situation. They are based on the house in the school grounds, and when not following (in school) those courses in which they have shown interest and readiness to work, they undertake activities in the school house and grounds such as gardening, cookery, typing or light craft. They were supervised by the headmaster and some senior teachers but a full-time warden (previously a youth tutor) has now been installed in a flat in the house and he has taken charge of these boys and girls. He visits their homes and encourages their parents to visit the school house: he works closely with the careers officer who specialises in the placement of the less able, and his wife (although not officially employed) makes a significant contribution. She is often able to establish a non-authoritarian relationship with the young people and has been known to offer a night's lodging and a 'cooling-off' period for those at loggerheads with their parents. It is not surprising to find that some boys and girls return to the house in the evening and at weekends to finish tasks that they have started during the day and that former pupils often visit the warden and his wife – sometimes with their girl or boy friends.

The schools with sixth forms of able pupils working for GCE advanced levels offer a wide range of subjects and timetable in such a way that combinations of arts and science subjects are possible. One example of a sixth form of 120 pupils studying 17 A-level subjects in 76 different combinations is typical of those schools with large sixth forms and a long tradition of advanced work. All give serious attention to general studies. One programme provides for religious education, the use of English and the BBC programmes, 'Prospect' and 'New Horizons', together with six units of study spread over two years. At present these comprise courses in the language of mathematics, the ideas of science, the use of literacy, introduction to sociology, the heritage of western civilisation, and government and law.

CONCLUSIONS

The conclusions of the enquiry were summarised in the final section under the headings of climate and leadership:

The schools visited differ in very many respects as institutions, although each can demonstrate its quality in its aims, in oversight of pupils, in curriculum design, in standards of teaching and academic achievements and in its links with the local community. What they all have in common is effective leadership and a 'climate' that is conducive to growth. The schools see themselves as places designed for learning: they take trouble to make their philosophies explicit for themselves and to explain them to parents and pupils; the foundation of their work and corporate life is an acceptance of shared values.

The messages of the Ten Good Schools enquiry remain as potent today as they were in 1975. Thus the junior education Minister speaking in 1987 recalled the report by HM Inspectorate which described good schools as places where

> ... emphasis is laid on consultation, team work and participation but, without exception, the most important single factor in the success of these schools is the quality of leadership of the head. ... without exception, the heads have qualities of imagination and vision, tempered by realism, which have enabled them to sum up not only the present situation but also attainable future goals.

CHAPTER 4

THE GREAT
EDUCATION DEBATE

James Callaghan's Ruskin College speech

The HMI discussion document *Ten Good Schools* appeared in unpublished form in 1976 and it was in this year that the Labour Government, under the leadership of James Callaghan, decided to renew earlier efforts to unlock the secret garden.

On this occasion the attempt was to be made, not immediately through the Department of Education and Science, but in the person of the Prime Minister himself.

Speaking at Ruskin College, Oxford, in October 1976, James Callaghan called for 'a Great Debate' with the aim of working towards a national consensus on educational aims and policies. This Governmental intrusion into the secret garden provoked considerable hostility at the time, since educational orthodoxy still demanded that all trespass into the garden should be prohibited: what should be taught and how it should be taught was none of central government's business.

Nevertheless, following the Ruskin College speech, a series of regional conferences was arranged throughout England and Wales, with the aim of bringing together teachers and parents along with representatives of the local education authorities and employers.

It was planned to codify the outcomes of these conferences in the form of a Green Paper and nudged by the Prime Minister and the Think Tank, the DES included in its final draft references to the desirability of some form of common core curriculum.

Education in Schools: A Consultative Document

In the event, Shirley Williams' Green Paper *Education in Schools: A Consultative Document* (1977) covered a wide range of educational topics including standards and assessment, transition between schools, and special needs of minority groups and the training of teachers.

On the question of the curriculum itself the consultative paper offered a detailed series of points for debate and action:

The principal points of concern appear to be:

(i) the curriculum has become overcrowded; the timetable is overloaded and the essentials are at risk;

(ii) variations in the approach to the curriculum in different schools can penalise a child simply because he has moved from one area to another;

(iii) even if the child does not move, variations from school to school may give rise to inequality of opportunities;

(iv) the curriculum in many schools is not sufficiently matched to life in a modern industrial society.

Not all these comments may be equally valid but it is clear that the time has come to try to establish generally accepted principles for the composition of the secondary curriculum for all pupils. This does not presuppose uniform answers: schools, pupils, and their teachers are different, and the curriculum should be flexible enough to reflect these differences. But there is a need to investigate the part which might be played by a "protected" or "core" element of the curriculum common to all schools. There are various ways this may be defined. Properly worked out, it can offer reassurances to employers, parents and the teachers themselves, as well as a very real equality of opportunity for pupils.

The creation of a suitable core curriculum will not be easy. Pupils in their later years of secondary schooling have a wide range of interests and expectations. Many of them will need help to see the relevance of what school offers and to understand how their skills can be used for their adult and working life. This can contribute to overcoming the lack of motivation and unco-operative attitudes displayed by some pupils. It is not the task of schools to prepare pupils for specific jobs but experience has long shown that studies and activities that are practical and obviously relevant to working life can be valuable as a means of learning, including the learning of basic skills.

Apart from the central question of curriculum planning up to the age of 16 there are other aspects of the problem that need more study.

(i) Some narrowing of the range of subjects studied after 16 is legitimate and perhaps inevitable, but traditional practice in England and Wales may have gone too far in this direction. Some of those who follow academic sixth form courses devote almost all their time to only two or three closely related subjects, without even the substantial broadening element of general studies provided in many schools. There has however been much discussion elsewhere of this feature of secondary education, and it will come under scrutiny again in relation to possible changes in the examination system.

(ii) Both before and after 16, care must be taken to see that girls do not by their choices limit the range of educational and career opportunities open to them. Positive steps may be necessary to encourage girls to broaden and modernise their aspirations and to feel confident of success in unfamiliar fields of science and technology. This is particularly important now that there are many fewer places available in colleges of education to which a large number of girls have traditionally gone for their higher education.

(iii) The curriculum for the less academic sixth former is not well defined. The same general principles apply as at earlier stages in the secondary school but particular care has to be taken to ensure that the education given to this very wide range of pupils furthers their career prospects as well as their personal development. It is important that they understand the range of opportunities open to them and what they stand to gain or lose by following one or other course.

Action on the curriculum

Action to improve the planning and development of the curriculum will be successful only if it takes into account fully the division of responsibilities for education in schools. The control of secular instruction in maintained schools – aided secondary schools apart – rests with the local education authority, subject to the provisions of each school's rules of management or articles of government. In practice, much of the responsibility for deciding the curriculum of each school is devolved by the local education authorities and the governors or managers upon the teachers or head teachers in the schools.

It would not be compatible with the duty of the Secretaries of State to 'promote the education of the people of England and Wales', or with their accountability to Parliament, to abdicate from leadership on educational issues which have become a matter of lively public concern. The Secretaries of State will therefore seek to establish a broad agreement with their partners in the education service on a framework for the curriculum, and, particularly, on whether, because there are aims common to all schools and to all pupils at certain stages, there should be a "core" or "protected part".

In their turn, the local education authorities must co-ordinate the curriculum and its development in their own areas, taking account of local circumstances, consulting local interests and drawing on the work of the Schools Council and other curricular research and development agencies. In this way the proper professional freedom of individual schools and their teachers can be exercised to the best advantage.

As the next step the Secretaries of State propose to invite the local authority and teachers' associations to take part in early consultations about the conduct of a review of curricular arrangements in each local authority area. The Schools Council will be invited to play a part in these consultations. Appropriate provision will also be made for other interested organisations to express their views.

The intention of the Secretaries of State is that, following these consultations, they should issue a circular asking all local education authorities to carry out the review in their own areas in consultation with their teachers and to report the results within about twelve months. The Departments would then analyse the replies as a preliminary to consultations on the outcome of the review and on the nature of any advice which the Secretaries of State might then issue on curricular matters.

The circular initiating the review would call for information about the existing practice of local education authorities and schools in their areas, and any plans already in hand for developing it. The following broad headings indicate the ground that the review is intended to cover:

- Local arrangements for the co-ordination of the curriculum and any plans for its development.
- The transition of pupils between schools.
- The keeping of school records of pupils' progress.
- Balance and breadth in the curriculum.
- Preparation for working life, including all aspects of schools/industry understanding and liaison and career education.
- The study of selected subject areas (eg English, mathematics, modern languages, science).

CHAPTER 5

CURRICULUM 11–16

These initial curriculum signals from the DES and HMI were couched in a general and hortatory form, but a working party of the inspectorate had simultaneously been developing a more detailed document under the title of *Curriculum 11–16*. Published in December 1977, this document consisted of a set of working papers on individual subject issues and was prefaced by three important introductory sections.

Section One dealt with the case for a common curriculum in secondary education from 11–16:

Changes in secondary education

The last twelve years have seen massive changes in secondary education, most obviously and notably as a consequence of reorganisation. The relatively simple pattern of grammar and modern schools which once widely prevailed has been succeeded by a 'patchwork quilt' of different types of local comprehensive scheme. By far the majority of pupils now attend comprehensive schools, but the schools themselves, though sharing common ideals, are more various than before in terms of size and age-range and style.

There has been necessary change, too, in the work that goes on inside them. Twelve years is a brief span in the history of an evolving national system, but it is the secondary school lifetime of eight generations of pupils. Teachers have found themselves needing to think through the curricular implications of reorganisation, together with the implications of the raising of the school-leaving age, even while the institutional changes are still being completed. The period has therefore seen markedly increased activity and acceleration of pace in curricular development, whether of the kind exemplified in the large projects of the Schools Council and other major agencies or in the explorations of individual schools and teachers.

On this busy educational map must also be superimposed the effects of population mobility: difficult though it is to make detailed and statistically up-to-date statements, such mobility is characteristic of advanced industrial societies and has to be taken into account in assumptions about children's learning experience.

Most secondary teachers now find themselves working in fairly recently constituted schools, generally larger than those they were used to before; many are dealing with an unaccustomed ability range among the pupils; the pupils themselves are, since 1973, at school for a year longer. Our society meanwhile has become noticeably more complex, and in many cases blurred in its perceptions of important issues. More and more responsibilites have been accepted by schools, particularly in matters of the personal and social welfare of pupils. During these same years a host of projects, schemes, proposals and suggestions about the curriculum has appeared. It is difficult to ascertain who has been influenced by what, and how, but teachers have been subject to a confusing series of propositions about what should or should not be done.

Acceptable and unacceptable variety

It is hardly surprising, therefore, that, in matters of the curriculum especially, variety is the order of the day. Such variety can reflect a healthy environment and vigorous and purposeful development in response to local need and opportunity; but equally it can be associated with an inadequate sense of direction and of priorities, with too little coordination both within and between schools, and with a reluctance to evaluate the curriculum offered as a whole. The contributory factors are many.

Schools have often been stimulated into changing their curricula and introducing new patterns of working, but many of the teachers concerned may have had little training or experience in planning such developments. It is, indeed, fair comment, we believe, that the hierarchical organisation of many secondary schools does not give the majority of teachers the sense and experience of being involved in fundamental educational thinking: decisions are often taken by the few and carried out by the many.

Or, schools may have operated in comparative isolation, picking up some ideas from outside, but largely having to learn from their own mistakes. The advice and teaching materials from major curriculum projects have not always made the expected contribution, and indeed there is so much on offer that to evaluate the findings and achievements presents schools with yet another problem. In too many cases, curriculum planning has been piecemeal – a matter of trying to cope with particular situations and problems as they arise rather than of developing a coherent programme based on a carefully thought out set of objectives, appreciated, understood and agreed upon by the whole staff.

Undoubtedly, too, a major obstacle to coherent development is the sense of 'autonomy' of the individual school, and often of the individual teacher in the classroom, and a deep reluctance to face the implications of partnership in curriculum planning. They nevertheless must be faced – and shared responsibility must be accepted.

It is doubtful if the country can afford – educationally as well as financially – the wasted effort, experiments embarked upon and left unfinished or unexamined, unnecessary repetitions, and most of all, the apparent lack of agreement on fundamental objectives. Indeed, all this is freely acknowledged in discussions all over the country by heads, teachers and administrators. Schools and administrators alike are anxious to do a good job, and there is concern about the bewildering diversity of practice, the problems of lack of balance within the curriculum, and the possibly adverse impact on pupils when unacceptable differences in the quality and range of educational experience offered result. The risks are recognised of inefficient use of resources, unnecessary fragmentation and lack of coordination. Much of the present unease and argument about education arises from a need to reconcile the right which a political democracy properly exercises in making local and national decisions on education with the considerable independence traditionally enjoyed by heads and teachers in determining how schools are run and what is taught, as well as how it is taught. Some common framework of assumptions is needed which assists coherence without inhibiting enterprise. Many heads and teachers will acknowledge this privately if not in public, and indeed often call for more drastic measures than we would think appropriate.

The 'core curriculum'

We indicated earlier why the approach to the curriculum most commonly found in schools is unlikely to satisfy the needs of pupils as we discern them. It is not particularly difficult to advocate and indeed to implement, given the appropriate resources, the notion of English, mathematics and science as a compulsory core for all pupils to 16. This, however, merely begins an educational discussion and does not provide a programme. What English? What mathematics? What science? If these are on the one hand compulsory, but on the other hand appropriately diversified in their objectives, content and methods of teaching, what exactly has been gained? Is this common enough? Or, indeed, is it a large enough common core to meet contemporary needs? We wish to put forward here for consideration a much broader curriculum for all pupils in secondary schools which would inevitably claim a substantial proportion of their time.

Towards a common curriculum

What have pupils a reasonable right to expect, given that they are obliged to be in school until they are 16? In the first place, without any doubt they have the right to expect to be enabled to take their place in society and in work, and this means that schools must scrutinise their curricula most carefully to see what is being done, by deliberate policies, to meet these expectations. Insofar as pupils may marry at 16, vote at 18, and become involved in legal responsibilities, what has the curriculum – the schools' deliberate educational policy – done to help them in these matters of fundamental importance to adult life? More than this, even though it may sound somewhat grandly put, pupils are members of a complicated civilisation and culture, and it is reasonable to argue that they have nothing less than a right to be introduced to a selection of its essential elements. Options systems may well prevent this from happening; the freedom to stop studying history, or art, or music, or biology at 14 means that pupils are not being given the introduction to their own cultural inheritance to which we believe they have a right. No one disputes the irrefutable case for basic skills and techniques; equally there is a case for cultural experiences and an introduction to values. There is also just as strong a case – less often acknowledged – for the formation of attitudes: to each other, to work, to obligations in society and not least to themselves. For themselves, pupils will need competence and an increasing sense of self-reliance, and the means whereby to develop a sense of integrity in the inevitably changing circumstances that await them.

It is for these reasons that our definition of a common curriculum is broad and makes substantial claims on time. We see that common curriculum as a body of skills, concepts, attitudes and knowledge, to be pursued, to a depth appropriate to their ability, by all pupils in the compulsory years of secondary education for a substantial part of their time, perhaps as much as two-thirds or three-quarters of the total time available. The remainder would be used either to deepen understanding of studies already in hand, or to undertake new activities, or both.

Definition of curriculum content

At this point, the working party attempted a definition of the content of the common core school curriculum: it was to be a curriculum which would occupy up to 75 per cent of pupils' time and it was not to rest upon a subject and subject content 'listing'. Instead it was maintained that underlying individual curriculum subjects were identifiable 'areas of experience'.

The actual subjects of the curriculum should, it was argued, contribute to a pupil's awareness of each of these areas of experience. For the sake of argument, the areas of experience were defined under eight separate headings, and as the debate continued, these headings came to be known as the 'eight adjectives':

Constructing a common curriculum

It is at this point that we come to the heart of our thesis. We see the curriculum to be concerned with introducing pupils during the period of compulsory schooling to certain essential 'areas of experience'. They are listed below in alphabetical order so that no other order of importance may be inferred: in our view, they are equally important.

Checklist

Areas of experience

The aesthetic and creative
The ethical
The linguistic
The mathematical
The physical
The scientific
The social and political
The spiritual

The list is not, or should not be, surprising; but the existing curricula of many pupils might well not measure up to it very satisfactorily. It does not in itself constitute an actual curricular programme. It is a checklist, one of many possible ones, for curricular analysis and construction. An advantage of such an approach is that many teachers would be rethinking what they know and do already, rather than beginning as novices in a new field. It does not in itself demand any one way of teaching or model of timetabling or pattern of internal school organisation. Given time for preliminary thinking and planning and the assembling and distribution of resources, it could be realised through a familiar-looking programme of single subjects, or through forms of interdisciplinary work, or with a combination of both; or it could lead to novel groupings and titles of studies. It does, of course, by enlarging the notion of a common 'core' to a curriculum that occupies the greater part of all pupils' time, put into question some types of 'option' scheme, though it does not deny the possibility of proper exercise of choice. The essential point to retain, in our view, is that any curriculum provided for pupils up to the age of 16 should be capable of demonstrating that it offers properly thought out and progressive experience in all these areas. Only so, we believe, can pupils' common curricular rights and society's needs be met.

None of the areas listed should be simply equated with a subject or a group of subjects, although obviously in some cases, e.g. the mathematical, a particular subject is recognisably the major contributor and means to learning. There is nothing essentially new in recognising that certain forms of learning experience, skills and concepts may be sought in a variety of curricular contexts: the Bullock report, *A language for life*, emphasised the importance of, but did not create, 'language across the curriculum' or the essential role of language in learning; the place of the aesthetic in mathematics or of the mathematical in music or geography has long been a familiar idea. Ethics does not normally appear as a separate and identifiable school course but it has a place in many sectors of the curriculum, wherever serious ethical questions need to be considered. Similarly, the spiritual aspects of human experience can be explored, for example, through art, music and drama as well as in say, history, literature and religion: but those planning the exploration need to know where they are going, and those engaged in it need to be helped to recognise what they have discovered.

45

It is also important to emphasise the fact that subject or 'course' labels often tell us surprisingly little about the objectives to be pursued or the activities to be introduced, still less about the likely or expected levels of achievement. An individual subject may make valid, although varied, contributions in different schools; or to different pupils in the same school; or to the same pupils at different ages or stages of individual development. Any framework to be constructed for the curriculum must be able to accommodate shifts of purpose, content and method in subjects, and of emphasis between subjects. In other words, it is not proposed that schools should plan and construct a common curriculum in terms of subject labels only: that would be to risk becoming trapped in discussions about the relative importance of this subject or that. Rather, it is necessary to look through the subject or discipline to the areas of experience and knowledge to which it may provide access, and to the skills and attitudes which it may assist to develop.

Definitions of curricular areas of experience

Initially, the simple listing of the 'eight adjectives' was regarded as sufficient to carry the argument forward.

In response to comment and criticism, however, the working party offered a closer definition of the 'intent' of the eight areas of experience, as follows:

Aesthetic and creative

The aesthetic area is concerned with an awareness of degrees of quality and an appreciation of beauty; the ability to perceive and respond both emotionally and intellectually to sensory experience; the knowledge and skills that may inform and enhance such experiences and their expression; the exploration and understanding of feeling and the conscious recognition of intuitive responses and action. The creative aspect is concerned with invention and may be the more active part of the aesthetic experience.

Ethical

The ethical area is concerned with principles underlying practical morality, descriptions of right and wrong conduct, obligations, duties and rights.

Linguistic

The linguistic area is concerned with the use of words in listening and reading, talking and writing. These activities help the individual to receive and process information, to enter the world of ideas, to make sense of his experience and to relate to others.

Mathematical

The mathematical area is concerned with familiarity with numbers and symbols and the ability to use them with confidence. It includes communicating, problem solving and generalising. Communicating means transmitting and interpreting information conveyed by tables, diagrams and models. Problem solving involves identifying the relevant variables in a real problem, setting up an abstract 'model' of the problem and using mathematical techniques to solve it. Generalising implies seeking and recognising patterns and relationships and justifying conclusions by logical argument expressed in precise and unambiguous language.

Physical

The physical area is concerned with awareness and understanding of the human body. It involves movement, through the development and maintenance of bodily skills, coordination and control, and manipulative abilities. Such experience of movement leads to an understanding of spatial dimensions and an appreciation of natural forces. Movement is a means of non-verbal communication, in which the individual may respond to a stimulus, drawing upon past experience and imagination.

Scientific

The scientific area is concerned especially with observing, predicting, and experimenting. Observing requires direct or indirect evidence from the physical world. Predicting will be based, consciously or unconsciously, on a hypothesis which explains patterns of previous observation. Predicting shows what will be the next most significant observation and its testing may require experimenting, the use of apparatus, physical skills, measurement and calculation.
Observing, predicting and experimenting do not merely make up the 'organised knowledge of the natural world' which is called science; they constitute a powerful method of problem solving.

Social/Political

The social and political area is concerned with relationships within society; between individuals, between individuals and social groups, and between social groups.
It involves a consideration of beliefs and values, of purposes and motivations, of rules and conventions, of authority and power.
Understanding one's own personal relationships requires self-knowledge as well as knowledge of and sensitivity towards others.

Spiritual

(i) The spiritual area is concerned with the awareness a person has of those elements in existence and experience which may be defined in terms of inner feelings and beliefs; they affect the way people see themselves and throw light for them on the purpose and meaning of life itself. Often these feelings and beliefs lead people to claim to know God and to glimpse the transcendent; sometimes they represent that striving and longing for perfection which characterises human beings but always they are concerned with matters at the heart and root of existence.

(ii) The spiritual area is concerned with everything in human knowledge or experience that is connected with or derives from a sense of God or of Gods. Spiritual is a meaningless adjective for the atheist and of dubious use to the agnostic. Irrespective of personal belief or disbelief, an unaccountable number of people have believed and do believe in the spiritual aspects of human life and therefore their actions, attitudes and interpretations of events have been influenced accordingly.

A landmark in the curriculum debate

The 11–16 Curriculum Papers of 1977, with their insistence on underlying curriculum structures, marked a considerable step forward in the detailed consideration of national curricular aims and objectives.

The general sections of the papers which have been considered here were complemented by individual subject statements. Burgeoning professional interest was indicated by the fact that over 34,000 copies of the 11–16 curriculum papers were distributed, on request: the concept of the eight areas of experience was carried forward into practical curriculum experiments and became an established landmark in the curricular scene.

CHAPTER 6

COMPREHENSIVE SCHOOLS AND MIXED ABILITY TEACHING

The problems

By 1978, considerable thought was being given not only to the content of the curriculum, but also to the methods of transmission of the curriculum, especially at secondary level.

A major criticism levelled at the comprehensive school system was that academic 'selection' had merely been transferred from *outside* the schools, to *inside* the schools. With a number on roll which could exceed a total of 2,000 pupils aged between 11 and 18 years, it was maintained that any organisational framework would demand the selection and grouping of pupils by ability bands, within the school itself.

Many schools saw a way out of the dilemma in a system of 'setting' pupils rather than complete streaming on an overall ability basis. In a 'setted' system, pupils from a heterogenous ability class separated into different groups according to their perceived strength in individual subjects. Thus for example, a pupil could appear in a 'top' set for modern languages and a 'middle' set for mathematics. The comprehensive principle and the administrative arrangements for year groups of pupils were preserved by continuing with a 'form' or 'class' system for pastoral aspects of the curriculum, including religious knowledge, for curriculum topics which might be less demanding in differentiated ability terms and for practical activities in the fields of art, music, PE and games.

A complementary approach lay in the reconsideration of the 'subject' titles themselves and their partial replacement by year group work in selected topics which spanned individual subject areas. This interdisciplinary or preferably crossdisciplinary 'topic' approach found considerable favour for first and second year pupils and the 'mixing' of subjects was often paralleled by a mixing of abilities in whole class groups.

Only by such mixed ability groupings, it was felt, could the comprehensive principle of valuing all human beings equally be achieved in practice. This was the view of many teachers as the comprehensive system developed and it demonstrated their attitudes of 'tolerance, patience and friendliness towards their pupils'.

But although the administrative arrangements for mixed ability *groupings* were easily implemented, the professional requirements for successful mixed ability *teaching* were not so readily achievable.

Mixed ability work in comprehensive schools

The 1978 HMI survey devoted a chapter to curriculum and teaching methods:

Curriculum

In each school seen there was in Years 1 to 3 a common curriculum for all pupils, with a reasonable range of subjects and experiences. The only field in which any options were likely to be generally offered was that of the aesthetic and practical subjects – art, craft, music and home economics. Sometimes a second foreign language was introduced in the third year and limited to pupils of linguistic ability; this had the effect of introducing an element of ability grouping into the organisation of that year. Some schools offered pupils, on entry, a choice between two alternative foreign languages, and constituted their groups accordingly; it was noticed that one or other of the languages might attract more able pupils.

Almost all the schools organised the work in the fourth and fifth years on lines that are common in secondary schools of all types. There was a common core of two or three subjects – usually including English and mathematics – studied by all pupils; in addition to these, pupils chose four or five optional subjects, with varying degrees of guidance and constraint. At this stage, the range of ability within some groups was likely to be less wide, as different subjects attracted pupils of particular abilities. While there was seldom a statement that mixed ability teaching formally ended after the third year, greater discretion was often given to subject departments to group pupils by ability at that stage if it seemed desirable in the pursuit of public examination objectives; and this was more likely to occur in the fifth year. Nevertheless, in English, humanities subjects, design and drama, mixed ability grouping continued for the full five years in a number of schools. This was rarer in mathematics, and very rare in science.

Syllabus content

There was a tendency for the same basic content to be offered to all pupils in mixed ability groups, the choice of material being determined by the needs of the large middle range of pupils. As a result there was often inadequate differentiation to meet the requirements of pupils of markedly differing abilities. In some subjects and areas of work attempts had been made to supplement basic content with extensions for the most able.

Other instances were found where a work guide provided pupils with indications of how they might select material appropriate to their capacities. In another case, tasks were chosen by the teacher from a resource bank but at the same time were selected in such a way that they followed a carefully structured plan of development suited to each pupil. In many instances encountered by HM Inspectors, mixed ability grouping had led to an extension of the range of content for pupils in the lower ability range; but it had often produced some restriction of experience for the most able which could lead to serious under-achievement.

Schemes of work, where they existed, did not on the whole make sufficient allowance for pupils being at widely different stages of development. Sometimes where consideration had been given to this aspect it had not been followed through in practice. Occasionally a subject department took the view that the collection of materials used was itself the scheme of work; this, however, left considerable areas of doubt about methodology and learning objectives. Many schemes were successful at identifying needs for appropriate learning materials and methods, but failed to identify clearly levels of expectation and attainment to be aimed at.

Teaching methods

The adoption of mixed ability grouping imposes the need to adopt teaching methods and modes of class management which are compatible with it. Methods which depend on the class being more or less homogeneous in ability clearly cannot succeed. A range of approaches, including whole class teaching, work in smaller groups, individual learning and individualised learning (see below), is necessary (any or all of these are usable and may be desirable with homogeneous groups, but they are not indispensable in that situation) if the varied needs of the pupils are to be met; though the balance between them will vary with the subject and the stage of learning.

Many mixed ability classes observed, however, demonstrated that the practice of having small groups of pupils working together for particular aspects of a subject was rarer than the whole class working together or the pupils working as individuals. Providing appropriate content and task, matching these to pupils in the small group, and ensuring that discussion which genuinely promoted learning took place seemed to have proved very difficult for many teachers. Where small groups were formed within the mixed ability class, their composition was usually self-determined by interest or friendship. Less commonly, the teacher selected group members either to ensure a spread of ability or to form more homogeneous groups. However, regrouping of pupils when this would have been appropriate within the mixed ability pattern was not often practised even when timetable facilities and accommodation were suitable or specially designed for this possibility. Certainly there was some lack of awareness of such possibilities, or of expertise in creating them. It may be that the need for such flexible grouping was sometimes obscured by the fact that the number of pupils at the extremes of the ability spectrum was comparatively small.

Whole class teaching was sometimes not utilised when it would have been the quickest, simplest, and most effective form of organisation and method. On the other hand, it was often over-employed in subjects such as mathematics, modern languages, English and the humanities, to a point where the wide differences between pupils which existed in mixed ability groups were seriously discounted. Some good class teaching which took full account of the range of ability was seen, however. For example, a class pursuing integrated studies in the humanities were presented with a film strip which gave opportunities for noting differences between present and past and making deductions. The teacher helped with sensitive questioning, and pupils of all abilities were able to contribute to and benefit from the work.

'Individual' and 'individualised' learning

The most frequent alternative to whole class teaching encountered during the survey was a situation in which pupils worked as individuals. This was often described as 'individualised learning'. In fact, a distinction needs to be recognised between individual work and individualised work. Individualised work involves personal assignments devised to meet the different needs, abilities, and attainments of individual pupils. Individual work is activity on which the pupil is engaged by himself, at his own pace, but which is essentially the same as that being undertaken by the rest of the class. Most of the work seen other than class teaching was individual rather than individualised.

Resource-based learning

In some cases, the pupils' experience was widened by individual learning based on the use of prepared resources, and their relationship with the teacher enriched by the associated experience of individual discussion with him. But in matters of motivation, pace, levels of difficulty and academic challenge, the hopes underlying resource-based methods had not often been realised. Sometimes resources were simply insufficient or unsuitable. In other cases their use was insufficiently exploited because of imprecise diagnosis of pupils' individual needs, lack of clear definition of learning objectives, and deficiencies in organisation within the classroom.

Resources produced by the schools

Some schools produced materials of very high quality for individual study, albeit at the cost of much time and energy. Since, however, some teachers lack the expertise to structure and write programmes and do not always have access to good graphics or good quality printing, some of the worksheets seen were visually unattractive and technically incompetent. In such circumstances, books and other material available commercially may be as or more effective.

Worksheets

At their best, worksheets discriminate between tasks, employ appropriate language and give clear guidance to pupils. Those used for geography in one school adopted different levels of approach to cater for the full ability range and provided full opportunity for the use of language in extended writing and summarising. But many of the examples seen failed to provide differentiation, confused pace of working with level of work by simply asking more able pupils to do more of the same in the available time, and did not offer problem solving opportunities. Many were unchallenging, lacking academic edge, creating a superficial attitude to learning, and failing to use a wide range of references to other sources of information and ideas. Weaker pupils were observed to have difficulty in meeting their demands on reading and writing skills.

Matching the methods to the group

Although in a few schools or departments within schools examples were found of effective and imaginative matching of methods to the problem of providing appropriately for all abilities in one teaching group, the general experience was otherwise.

HMIs' CONCLUSION

The crux of the problem of teaching methods in a mixed ability school organisation was aptly summarised in the concluding sentences of the section:

> 'While we found . . . mixed ability grouping, we had greater difficulty in finding mixed ability teaching'. Predominantly, the whole class was offered the same experience, whether by being taught as one group or by being set the same insufficiently differentiated tasks to perform as individuals.

THE 19 SALIENT POINTS

The effects of mixed ability grouping were summarised in the survey under a total of 19 important points:

1. Generally, mixed ability grouping was associated with good relationships between pupils and between teachers and pupils, and with coopera-

tive attitudes on the part of the pupils. Often a high level of motivation was engendered among pupils of below average ability. Standards of courtesy were above those commonly encountered; and it was understood that, where pupils of lower ability had formerly been grouped together in Years 4 and 5, the incidence of disruptive behaviour in this age group had been reduced following the adoption of mixed ability grouping. There were, however, a few cases where mixed ability grouping had resulted in a wider distribution of disruptive behaviour.

2. In a very small number of schools, pupils were working at an appropriate pace and level in all the subjects and year-groups to which mixed ability organisation applied; and in others there was excellent work in some subject areas.

3. In most of the schools visited, however, HM Inspectors felt concern about the level, pace and scope of the work in a significant number of subjects. This concern was sometimes on behalf of pupils of all abilities; more frequently it related to the extremes of the ability range; most frequently it related to the most able pupils.

4. In a number of schools where their special needs were understood and met the less able pupils seemed to be doing better in mixed ability classes in subjects where learning was not markedly sequential. They benefited from the stimulus of working among pupils more able than themselves.

5. Many programmes of work did not provide for differences of ability. Since they were often drawn up with the average in mind, pupils of average ability were the best served in such circumstances. But even the needs of the average had not always been accurately assessed and provided for.

6. Most frequently it was pupils of well above average ability who were not adequately catered for. For them, low expectation by teachers and failure to provide appropriate work programmes resulted in under-achievement.

7. Failure to diagnose under-achievement and to recognise individual needs sometimes stemmed from the fact that the teachers' commitment to the mixed ability principle was accompanied by reluctance to assess and record pupils' progress on the grounds that such processes were associated with competitiveness and with a system of grading inconsistent with the equal valuing of all pupils.

8. In a few schools, teaching methods had been matched to the problem of providing appropriately for all abilities in one teaching group. In most, they had not; and mixed ability groups did not receive mixed ability teaching.

9. More often than not teachers resorted either to whole-class teaching or to a system of individual (but not necessarily individualised) learning, and did not exploit sufficiently the possible variants between these extremes which could meet the needs of mixed ability classes.

10. In some schools, the development of resource-based learning for mixed ability classes was resulting in a greater variety of learning approaches. However, the great reliance placed on the worksheet as the main basis of individual learning had significant drawbacks. It overemphasised the transfer of information, encouraged intellectual conformity rather than questioning attitudes and the capacity for independent thinking, and developed writing skills at the expense of oral ones. Some pupils complained of boredom and a feeling of isolation produced by too much individual working.

11. Mixed ability organisation had often resulted in some restriction of content in programmes of work. Sometimes teachers avoided topics or activities deemed too difficult for pupils of average ability or below, or difficult to present to mixed ability groups.

12. The quality of the educational process was adversely affected where teachers were faced with the difficulties of teaching 'integrated studies' in addition to the difficulties of teaching mixed ability groups.

13. The majority of pupils exhibited at least a satisfactory attitude to work. Where this was not so, the cause usually appeared to be the provision of unsuitable work or the use of unsuitable teaching methods.

14. With a lack of variety in the classroom approach and with failure to provide suitably differentiated programmes, mixed ability grouping often resulted in uniformity in the level and pace of work, usually pitched at pupils of average ability or below. The combination of a slow pace and an undemanding level of work led not only to under-achievement but to some frustration for some pupils by the time they had reached the third year.

15. The presence of abler pupils in well taught groups seemed to improve the work attitudes of pupils of average and lower ability. Where there were few able pupils in a group, however, they themselves appeared to suffer because of a lack of stimulus.

16. Analysis of public examination results threw little light on the effectiveness of mixed ability work because other factors affected the issue.

17. There was a tendency in the fourth and fifth years to concentrate narrowly on preparation for public examinations in order to make up for a slow pace in earlier years.

18. In schools that retained mixed ability grouping in the fourth and fifth years, there was a steady development of courses leading to CSE Mode 3 examinations.

19. Schools with mixed ability organisation had attracted many dedicated teachers who made great efforts to ensure its effectiveness. It was clear, that the teaching of mixed ability groups made greater demands than more traditional forms of teaching.

For a mixed ability programme to achieve its objectives and be fully effective both educationally and socially, adequate and detailed consideration needs to be given to the full implications of the adoption of the policy:

1. It is unwise for a school to make a blanket decision on the introduction of mixed ability organisation. For each subject and for each year-group the reasons for adopting it should be more carefully weighed, and the likely consequences considered.

2. The decision to adopt mixed ability organisation should be taken for positive rather than negative reasons, and not merely in the hope that a new situation will produce new thinking.

3. Social and educational considerations should be kept in proper balance.

4. Careful consideration should be given not only to whether a mixed ability organisation is desirable, but to whether the teachers in the school or department are capable of coping with it without detriment to the interests of the pupils.

5. Schools, and departments within them, should carefully consider whether their accommodation and resources are suitable for mixed ability work, or can be made so.

6. Adequate time should be allowed to prepare thoroughly for a change to mixed ability methods.

7. For the whole school and for individual subject departments, clear written statements should be made of the aims and objectives to be worked for through mixed ability organisation, and of the methods by which these may be achieved.

8. The adoption of mixed ability grouping imposes a need to adopt teaching methods and modes of class management which are compatible with it. Appropriate teaching strategies should be developed to meet the needs of the wide ability range within each mixed ability group. Programmes for the various levels of ability should be adequately differentiated

and, for all categories of pupil, should have both quality and variety. The amount of time to be devoted to individual working merits special consideration.

9. Preparations for teaching mixed ability groups demand substantially more of the teacher's time than preparation for teaching more homogeneous groups.

10. Schools should consider whether their staffing situation and their overall curricular policies are such that mixed ability groups can be kept to a manageable size without imposing undue strains on teachers or on other aspects of provision.

11. The adoption of mixed ability methods has implications for the whole five year course, at the end of which most pupils take public examinations. The pace and content of the first two years should be carefully monitored and the transition from work in the earlier years to work for public examinations carefully considered.

12. Particular attention has to be paid to the assessing and recording of pupils' progress. Assessment is more difficult where mixed ability grouping is used; but it is essential in order to ensure that the programme for each pupil is appropriate.

13. At whole school and at departmental level, teachers should regularly question the results of their work. Programme content and methods of working should be frequently reviewed to assess their effectiveness.

14. For a system of individual working to be fully effective, a plentiful supply and a wide variety of appropriate resources are needed. The production and evaluation of these, their use and storage and retrieval arrangements have all to be thoughtfully organised.

15. Institutions for the initial training of teachers should take account of the possibility that their students may subsequently find themselves teaching mixed ability groups.

16. If teachers are to meet the complex demands of mixed ability teaching, appropriate in-service training should be provided.

17. Sufficient ancillary help is necessary so that the production and preparation of resources for mixed ability teaching does not unduly consume the time and energy of teachers.

18. LEA advisory services have a significant part to play in helping schools to review the results of mixed ability work and in in-service training.

QUALITY OF TEACHING

As always, the quality of the teaching force constitutes an overriding factor in the success or failure of the organisational plan:

> *Mixed ability teaching requires special qualities in the teachers involved. Catering adequately for the full ability range within each mixed ability group calls for more sophisticated professional skills than does teaching in more traditional forms of organisation.*

CONCLUSIONS

The concluding comment in the survey stressed that:

> *With mixed ability classes perhaps more than with other forms of grouping, it is necessary for teachers to plan not only the content of lessons but also the organisation of time and pupil contact.*

Such planning implies good departmental leadership, careful assessment of the children's progress and due attention to the wider aspects of the educational enterprise including such factors as the place of homework in curriculum planning and the involvement of parents and the local community in the overall strategies of a school.

CHAPTER 7

THE CURRICULUM DOCUMENTS TRILOGY

A Framework for the School Curriculum

In 1979 a Conservative Government was returned to power under the leadership of Margaret Thatcher, and a year later the new Secretary of State for Education and Science, Mark Carlisle, re-opened the issues of the Great Debate with curricular proposals under the heading of a consultative paper entitled *A Framework for the School Curriculum*.

This paper was the first in a trilogy of central documents of the early 1980s, and it stressed a division of responsibility for the school system between central government and the local education authorities. The paper declared that each education authority should have clear and known policies for the curriculum offered in its schools, and should plan for future development accordingly in consultation with teachers in the schools.

The 'Framework' paper went on to maintain that because of *diversity in practice* in schools, it was 'timely' to *prepare guidance on the place which certain key elements of the curriculum should have in the experience of every pupil*.

Returning to the concept of a core curriculum, the paper pointed out that:

In the course of the public and professional debate about the school curriculum a good deal of support has been found for the idea of identifying a 'core' or essential part of the curriculum which should be followed by all pupils according to their ability. Such a core, it is hoped, would ensure that all pupils, whatever else they do, at least get a sufficient grounding in the knowledge and skills which by common consent should form part of the equipment of the educated adult.

Thus expressed, the idea may appear disarmingly simple; but as soon as it is critically examined a number of supplementary questions arise. For example, should the core be defined as narrowly as possible, or should it, for the period of compulsory schooling at least, cover a large part of the individual's curriculum? Should it be expressed in terms of the traditional school subjects, or in terms of educational objectives which may be attained through the medium of various subjects, appropriately taught? The difficulties and uncertainties attached to the application of the core concept do not mean, however, that it may not be a useful one in carrying forward the public debate about the curriculum to the point at which its results can be of practical benefit to the schools.

The 'Framework' paper identified the places of English, mathematics, science, modern languages, religious education and physical education in a proposed core curriculum. The worm of centralist prescription emerged in the further declaration that the Secretaries of State considered that all pupils should devote specific amounts of time to each of the common core elements. This was to be in the region of 10 per cent of the timetable per subject in the early years of a secondary school course, rising to 20 per cent for some subjects (e.g. science and modern languages) after the age of 13.

A view of the curriculum

The 'Framework' paper referred to the contribution of the HMI 11–16 documents and the 'eight areas of experience' and for a 'fuller statement about the curriculum' it pointed readers to a new HMI document which also appeared in 1980. This document, entitled *A View of the Curriculum* was issued as No 11 in the *Matters for Discussion* series. In the Introduction, the paper commented upon the two seemingly contrary requirements of the curriculum.

On the one hand the curriculum must reflect the broad aims of education which apply to all children. On the other hand it is necessary to consider the differences in ability and interests of children of the same chronological age. Hence the important point was made that any broadly based concept of a common core curriculum must be tempered by a regard for individual curricular programmes in order to reflect year by year the individual as well as the common needs of pupils.

Underlying the traditional subject catalogue of the curriculum, the paper reiterated that there were essential areas of understanding and experience which should serve as a check list in constructing the curricular blocks of the school timetable.

Other important considerations which must bear upon a view of the curriculum were said to revolve around questions of standards and expectations of continuity in education, of public demands upon schools and a regard for 'the limits of the possible'.

On the topic of the curriculum in primary schools, the paper offered a fairly optimistic view:

Current practice is such that discussion on the primary school curriculum does not need to concern itself so much with the total range of the work as with the extent to which parts of the curriculum are developed, especially for the more able children. It is only provision of observational and experimental science that is seriously lacking in many primary schools; and the teaching of French that is sometimes attempted when conditions are not suitable. More extensive discussion is required on the levels to which work could and should be taken, at least for some children, in the various parts of the curriculum; for example, the identification of the skills and ideas associated with geography and history that are suitable for primary school children should help teachers to ensure that the day-to-day programme is organised so that children become acquainted with these skills and ideas, and should help to improve continuity from one class or school to the next – whether or not these subjects are shown separately on the timetable. Working parties of teachers, LEA advisers, inspectors and others have already shown what useful guidelines can be produced for parts of the curriculum, particularly, but not only, in mathematics.

Anxiety is sometimes expressed that maintaining a wide curriculum in primary schools may be possible only at the expense of the essential, elementary skills of reading, writing and mathematics. The evidence from the HMI survey of primary education in England does not bear out that anxiety. A broad curriculum can include many opportunities for the application and practice of the skills of reading, writing and calculating. It should be planned to include them, and every opportunity should then be taken to improve children's abilities in these essential skills.

At secondary level, the paper maintained the task of common core curriculum planning became much more difficult:

There is apparently no guarantee that five years of secondary education will have provided the pupil with opportunities to acquire, at whatever level, skills or knowledge or forms of understanding universally acknowledged as important. Happily the realities are not quite so anarchic, because habit and common sense ensure that schools, in practice, are not so divergent as the lack of any explicit common curricular philosophy might suggest. Nevertheless, there are sufficient grounds for unease to suggest a need to re-examine the rationale and organisational structure of the prevailing curriculum in many secondary schools.

The 'Propositions'

For logical and sustained progress in the curriculum tangle to be made, it was regarded as necessary to consider a number of 'propositions'. In summary, these were:

1. There is a need for a greater and much more explicit consensus nationally on what constitutes five years of secondary education up to the age of 16.

2. 'Secondary education for all' entails that the formal curriculum should offer all pupils opportunities to engage in a largely comparable range of learning.

3. Within the education system as a whole, locally and nationally, there should be comparable opportunities and comparable quality, though not uniformity, of education for all pupils in all schools.

4. There is need for cohesion between education up to 16 and that which follows after.

5. There is need for more coherence within the experience of individual pupils, and this requires conscious policies, appropriate structures, effective planning and careful evaluation on the part of the schools and their teachers.

6. Since most of the learning takes place through the study of traditional subjects, it is essential that those who teach them and who design schemes of work should identify explicitly the knowledge and skills each of those studies is expected to promote and examine their combined significance for the education of individual pupils.

7. Extending the amount of common ground implies in practice a broader coverage of subjects than many pupils now sustain to the age of 16, and a substantially larger compulsory element in the final two years.

8. In any future development of the curriculum, to those elements already widely held in common – English, mathematics, religious education, physical education – should certainly be added some continued form of science education for all pupils.

9. There is also a strong case for a modern language in the education of all pupils, and for the establishment of national policy on the place of individual languages in the system.

10. No pupils' programmes should be wholly deficient in the arts and applied crafts.

11. There is, in particular, a strong case for maintaining some study of history in the final secondary years.

12. It is also certain that schools need to secure for all pupils opportunities for learning particularly likely to contribute to personal and social development.

13. In a curriculum designed to include a substantially larger compulsory programme than now, common to all pupils, there would still be room and need for differentiation and choice. In the compulsory part there is need within broad subject fields to differentiate levels of work, content and emphasis.

14. The 'optional' sector should provide the necessary opportunities to take up new or additional subjects, or to encounter new elements of experience or knowledge not contained within the compulsory curriculum, or to give time to extend or reinforce compulsory studies, where some pupils with learning difficulties will need continued help.

CONCLUSIONS
In its conclusion, the *View of the Curriculum* document stressed again the need for a broad curriculum, with a '*substantially larger compulsory element*'.
It was suggested that a fairly lengthy process of consultation would be required, both locally and nationally:

> To establish broad policies on the structure of the curriculum as a whole, and to develop a range of documents further defining the parts of the curriculum and their relationship to each other.

The school curriculum

The final contribution in the curriculum trilogy appeared a year later, when in March 1981 the DES returned once more to the topic of what should be taught in schools. In *The School Curriculum* it reiterated its conception of the 'broad educational aims' offered in the consultative paper of 1980. It stressed the view that it was for individual schools to 'shape the curriculum for each pupil' and stated unequivocally that *'neither the government nor the local authorities should specify in detail what the schools should teach.'* Signals were nevertheless given on the importance of school governing bodies, the need to provide a forum for bringing together teachers, parents and the local community and the curricular importance of the public examination system.

THE 'RECOMMENDED APPROACH'

A *Recommended Approach* with its implications at both primary and secondary levels was detailed in the paper, and this 'Recommended Approach' outlined the key questions which in the view of the Secretaries of State each school should pursue.

At primary level:

Within limits both detailed curricula and the teaching approaches used will properly vary from school to school according to the strengths of the teachers and local circumstances. Within classes, teachers have to be sensitive to the different abilities and interests of children both as a group and as individuals so that the range and pace of the programme are appropriate. An approach which may be suitable for an able child – for example through a relatively sophisticated use of language – may be beyond the understanding of a less able child: to treat both alike would be an injustice to one or both.

Primary schools rightly attach high priority to English and mathematics. This is an overriding responsibility: it is essential that the early skills in reading, writing and calculating should be effectively learned in primary schools, since deficiencies at this stage cannot easily be remedied later and children will face the world seriously handicapped. The schools must, however, provide a wide range of experience, in order to stimulate the children's interest and imagination and fully to extend pupils of all abilities. There is no evidence that a narrow curriculum, concentrating only on the basic skills, enables children to do better in these skills: HM Inspectors' survey suggests that competence in reading, writing and mathematics may be improved where pupils are involved in a wider programme of work and if their skills in language and mathematics are applied in a variety of contexts.

This wider curriculum should incorporate certain key elements. Children should be encouraged, in the context of the multi-cultural aspects of Britain today and of our membership of the European Communities, to develop an understanding of the world, of their own place in it and of how people live and work. This involves, certainly for the more able children and in a simpler form for many others, an introduction to the concepts of history, such as chronology and cause and effect, and to the weighing of evidence from different sources; opportunity to become acquainted with written material of different types, and to learn to distinguish fact from fiction; some understanding of the geography of their home area and of more distant places; and an appreciation of religious beliefs and practices. In addition, children's curiosity about their physical and natural environment should be exploited; all pupils should be involved in practical as well as theoretical work in elementary science, to develop skills of observation and recording. These skills can be further enhanced, and children introduced to different ways of recording and interpreting experience, through aesthetic and practical subjects such as art and craft and physical education. Music, both instrumental and vocal, contributes to children's development in a similar way. Finally, schools are concerned with the personal and social development of their pupils in the widest sense; they need to foster, in their approaches to the curriculum, children's developing awareness of themselves as individuals and of the way in which they relate to others.

Most primary schools already incorporate most or all of these elements in their curricula; deficiencies occur less often as a matter of policy than where space is short or teaching expertise lacking. What is now needed is to develop a good deal of what is common practice in a more demanding way, particularly in order to ensure that challenging work is provided for the ablest. Schools should stimulate the more able children to acquire and make use of books, other reference sources and original data in ways that suit the occasion: their teachers should more than is now common expect the older pupils to observe and classify, to make simple generalisations, to appreciate inter-relations, and to arrive at and test their own ideas.

At secondary level, the School Curriculum paper formulated three principal propositions for consideration:

1. Schools should plan their curriculum as a whole. The curriculum offered by a school, and the curriculum received by individual pupils, should not be simply a collection of separate subjects; nor is it sufficient to transfer, with modifications, the ideas about the curriculum in the separate selective and non-selective schools of an earlier generation into the comprehensive schools attended by most pupils today.

2. There is an overwhelming case for providing all pupils between 11 and 16 with curricula of a broadly common character, designed so as to ensure a balanced education during this period and in order to prevent subsequent choices being needlessly restricted.

3. School education needs to equip young people fully for adult and working life in a world which is changing very rapidly indeed.

The concluding sections of the School Curriculum paper offered some generalised suggestions on specific areas of the curriculum.

The dominant plea, nevertheless, was summarised for the trilogy of curriculum papers in one paragraph:

Although choices are made, and have to be made, at the end of the third year, every pupil up to 16 should sustain a broad curriculum. The level, content and emphasis of work will be related to pupils' abilities and aspirations, but there should be substantial common elements. These should include English and mathematics, whose vital importance schools already recognise in the time and attention they devote to them. To these should be added science, religious education and physical education; in addition, pupils should undertake some study of the humanities designed to yield lasting benefit and should retain opportunities for some practical and some aesthetic activity. Most pupils should study a modern language, and many should continue to do so through the whole five-year period. Within all this there should still be room for choice, so that all pupils can give expression to their aptitudes and interests in taking up additional subjects or reinforcing their largely common programmes.

CHAPTER 8

A CURRICULUM EXPERIMENT

The 1977 proposals paper which followed James Callaghan's Great Debate, the 11–16 HMI Curriculum papers, the 'Framework' paper of 1980 and the HMI and DES Curriculum statements of 1980 and 1981 were all at a consultative and discussion level.

In order to make practical progress in the curriculum tangle however, it was essential to try out the proposed curriculum ideas in real situations. This practical dimension had already been envisaged as a necessity by the Inspectorate following the issue of the 11–16 Curriculum working papers in 1977. It was therefore decided to invite LEAs to participate in a curriculum experiment with the involvement of HMI and local authority advisers.

In the event, five LEAs and a total of 41 schools contributed to a joint curricular enquiry concerned with 'the reality of the curriculum for real pupils in real schools'.

Curriculum 11–16: A Statement of Entitlement

Monitoring the work of the experiment which was christened 'Curriculum re-appraisal in action' commenced in 1979. Two years later a progress report was published and a final report appeared in 1983 under the title of *Curriculum 11–16: A Statement of Entitlement*.

The case study reports outlined in what came to be known as the 'Red Book' documents illustrated both the rewards and the difficulties – 'warts and all' – involved in joint curricular action involving schools, local authorities, advisers and inspectors.

The most enduring result was encapsulated in the case which was made for an 'entitlement' curriculum.

Thus, in Chapter 3 of the final report it was noted that:

The conviction has grown that all pupils are entitled to a broad compulsory common curriculum to the age of 16, which introduces them to a range of experiences, makes them aware of the kind of society in which they are going to live and gives them the skills necessary to live in it. Any curriculum which fails to provide this balance and is overweighted in any particular direction, whether vocational, technical or academic, is to be seriously questioned. Any measures which restrict the access of all pupils to a wide-ranging curriculum or which focus too narrowly on specific skills are in direct conflict with the entitlement curriculum envisaged.

THE INDISPENSABLE ELEMENTS

It was pointed out that the specification for such a curriculum would contain a number of indispensable elements including the following:

(i) A statement of aims relating to the education of the individuals and to the preparation of young people for life after school.

(ii) A statement of objectives in terms of skills, attitudes, concepts and knowledge.

(iii) A balanced allocation of time for all the eight areas of experience (the aesthetic and creative; the ethical; the linguistic; the mathematical; the physical; the scientific; the social and political; and the spiritual) which reflects the importance of each and a judgement of how the various component courses contribute to these areas.

(iv) Provision for the entitlement curriculum in all five years for all pupils of 70–80 per cent of the time available with the remaining time for various other components to be taken by pupils according to their individual talents and interests.

(v) Methods of teaching and learning which ensure the progressive acquisition by pupils of the desired skills, attitudes, concepts and knowledge.

(vi) A policy for staffing and resource allocation which is based on the curriculum.

(vii) Acceptance of the need for assessment which monitors pupils' progress in learning, and for explicit procedures, accessible to the public, which reflect and reinforce (i) and (v) above.

THE PRACTICAL IMPLICATIONS

Finally, it was observed that the adoption of an entitlement curriculum would have considerable practical implications for school timetabling and course planning:

What might the entitlement look like in terms of timetables and courses? The way in which time is allocated is crucial. Given the wide nature of the curriculum, it is unlikely that its common elements can be achieved in less than 75 per cent of the time available in all of the five years of secondary schooling 11 to 16. This leaves about 25 per cent of the time for other courses to which children are also entitled and which would differ according to individual needs, ambitions and interests. The entitlement curriculum raises fundamental questions about the way in which time is allocated. It necessarily questions the inherited ideas about time in the curriculum. If the areas of experience are important it is necessary that all are seen to be important in the timetable. For example, do mathematics or English or a modern language have to be allocated five periods per week over five years as in traditional timetabling practices, while music and religious education have only one period? Is there any point at all in allocating a subject one period only? Do subjects have to be taught continuously over a five year span even for public examinations? For example, does history or geography have to be taught in every term, in every year, of a five year curriculum with a small allocation of two or three periods a week? Is there a case for a modular system by which, for example, history might be taught in one year or term with six periods a week and not at all in another? Is it always necessary to divide the day into small portions of time, such as eight thirty-five minute periods? This practice is based upon a teacher-centred model of learning in which instruction dominates and pupil concentration spans are assumed to be limited. If another model is envisaged in which pupils are more actively involved in learning and where social skills such as discussion and cooperation are being encouraged, would not longer portions of time, at least in some parts of the week, become essential?

It is not easy to restructure the timetable. Schools which have attempted it have usually confined it to years 1–3 or to the timetables of less able pupils, partly because of the concern not to jeopardise examination results of 16-plus. The difficulties involved are real but the timetable should be seen as a means to an end, translating into practice as closely as possible the principles it has been decided should underpin the curriculum. If, for example, a curriculum based on the eight areas of experience were adopted, it might be necessary to work through a process similar to that suggested in Appendix 3 (curriculum models) before arriving at an apportionment of time to subjects. If a wider common curriculum is to be achieved, then subject time allocations and fixed timetable patterns cannot remain sacrosanct.

There are also implications for the subjects and courses which make up the curriculum. In addition to the traditional subjects, it is likely that new courses will be needed. For example, while history, geography, sociology and social studies may all contribute to political and social awareness, it is possible that a purpose-built combined studies course with a new name, at some point in a five year curriculum, could be a more effective way of helping pupils to gain this kind of understanding. Similarly a separate course in personal development (or some similar name) may be one way of giving pupils the skills, attitudes, concepts and knowledge relating to adult life in terms of education for health, for parenthood, for employment and independent living. However, even the introduction of new courses will not guarantee that all aims are achieved and schools should establish procedures to check what pupils are receiving. Apart from new courses, the place of traditional subjects will need to be reconsidered. For example, if language is developed across the curriculum, what then is the precise function of English and will it need an allocation of six periods a week?

Should its function be conceived more as that of introducing children to literature? Or if the aim is a worthwhile scientific experience for all pupils in a common curriculum to 16, are separate courses in three sciences the most appropriate way to achieve this? If one aim is to give all pupils a worthwhile linguistic experience, what is the value of most current practice in the teaching of a modern language? Certainly the range of the common curriculum for all pupils up to 16 would prevent the inclusion of, say, additonal sciences or a second modern language for any pupils; these would have to be included in the 25 per cent of the time outside that needed for the common curriculum, and in the time available for post-16 education. Such considerations reinforce a point already made that new examinations will be necessary. If the adoption of the entitlement curriculum involves the development of new shorter modular courses, and shorter option courses, then current public examinations which expect, for example, four or five years study of French up to 16 would not be suitable, although graded tests might provide an appropriate means of assessment and certification.

The curriculum of every school should develop pupils' awareness of the democratic multi-cultural society in which they live, the competitive nature of the world of industry and commerce, the implications of recent technological advances. There must equally be provision for the development of personal and social skills including health education and education for parenthood; for some appreciation of the realities of unemployment and increased leisure time and for developing some understanding of career opportunities in the context of future patterns of working life. All these developments require cross-curricular work. The enquiry has found that in some schools this has been achieved by establishing new courses and in others by ensuring effective coordination across the subjects in the curriculum. Whatever the way adopted to achieve it, all these elements must be part of that common curriculum which occupies 70–80 per cent of the available time if pupils are to be equipped to face the demands of adult society. Any more specific courses, whether academic or vocational, must take place in the time remaining.

It is clear that the entitlement curriculum demands that schools consider very carefully not only the courses but also the time allocated to each of them. It cannot be assumed that a satisfactory vehicle for such a curriculum already exists in either traditional subject titles or time allocations.

CHAPTER 9

STANDARDS AND ACHIEVEMENTS IN SCHOOLS

In the years following the Great Debate of 1976 both the Government and the DES had attempted sporadically to pull existing educational levers in the cause of the curriculum. Success had been very limited even after the publication in 1980 of the Conservative Government's *Framework for the Curriculum*. But by 1984 the new Secretary of State, Sir Keith Joseph, had become determined to adopt a much more interventionist stance.

Sir Keith Joseph's North of England 1984 speech

Speaking at the North of England Education Conference in 1984, he announced government plans:

(a) To define the objectives of the main parts of the 5–16 curriculum so that everyone knows the level of attainment that should be achieved at various stages by pupils of different abilities;
(b) To alter the 16+ examinations so that they measure absolute, rather than relative, performance;
(c) To establish, as a realistic objective, the aim of bringing 80–90 per cent of all pupils *at least* to the level which is now expected and achieved in the 16+ examinations by pupils of average ability in individual subjects; and to do so over a broad range of skills and competences in a number of subjects.

As examples of the proposed minimum level to be attained at 16, Sir Keith declared that:

'In English*, pupils would need to demonstrate that they are attentive listeners and confident speakers when dealing with everyday matters of which they have experience. That they can read straightforward written information and pass it on without loss of meaning, and that they can say clearly what their own views are.'

'*In mathematics*, that they understand, and can apply, the topics and skills in the foundation list proposed in the Cockcroft Report.'

'*In science*, that they are willing and able to take a practical approach to problems involving sensible observations and appropriate measurements, and can communicate their findings effectively, that they can put information to good use in making sensible predictions from the regularities and patterns which they perceive, and that they can act on instructions presented in a variety of ways and can follow safety procedures.'

'*In history*, that they possess some historical knowledge and perspective, understand the concept of cause and consequence, and can compare and extract information from historical evidence and be aware of its limitations.'

'*In craft, design and technology*, that they can design and make something using a limited range of materials and calling on a restricted range of concepts and give an account of what they have done and the problems they encountered.'

The Secretary of State further maintained that four principles should be observed in the planning and execution of the primary and secondary curriculum:

'*First* it should be broad for all pupils both in the development of personal qualities and in the range of knowledge and skills to which pupils are introduced. That means, for example, that every primary pupil should be properly introduced to science; and that secondary pupils should not drop subjects in the fourth and fifth years in a way which leaves them insufficiently equipped for subsequent study or training.'

'*Second*, the curriculum should be relevant to the real world and to the pupils' experience of it. Judged by that test, HMI reports show that much of what pupils are now asked to learn is clutter. The test means, for example, that the curriculum should contain an adequate practical element and promote practical capability for all pupils, not just for those who are labelled 'non-academic'; that the technical and vocational aspect of school learning should have its proper place, and that all pupils should be introduced to the economic and other foundations of our society.'

'*Third*, there should be differentiation within the curriculum for variations in the abilities and aptitudes of pupils. This is a task that has to be tackled within each school as well as between schools, where this is relevant.'

'*Fourth*, the various elements of the curriculum need to be balanced in such a way as to optimise the contribution that each can make to the total education of the pupil. Insofar as each main element does something for the pupil that no other element does, or does as well, no pupil should miss the chance of getting out of each such element the special competence and understanding which it helps him to acquire.'

For these principles to be attained nationally, there needed to be:

An explicit definition of the objectives of each phase and of each subject area of the curriculum.

On the question of examinations, Sir Keith maintained that new curricula and higher standards would call for a reform of the existing examination system. In particular Sir Keith pointed out that:

'We need: a reasonable assurance that pupils obtaining a particular grade will know certain things and possess certain skills or have achieved a certain competence – in other words we need to move towards a system of grade-related criteria . . .

The requirements for the award of each grade to be no lower than the level of attainment which can be broadly associated with the corresponding grades in the existing system, for example the O level Grade C.'

Finally, Sir Keith remarked upon the schools' need to develop personal qualities:

'We expect schools to be concerned with the behaviour of pupils and with the code by which the pupils live; and to create a model of how people should relate to one another which will guide and fortify their pupils now and later. I believe we are right in thinking this an important aspect of standards in schools. But the schools are not on their own in this. Parents have a crucial part to play.'

The abolition of the Schools Council

As if to illustrate the Government's determination to take over the educational reins, it was finally decided in the same year that the existing central forum for educational discussion and course development, namely the Schools Council, should be abolished. Since its inception in 1964, the Council during its existence had had to face problems of lack of authority, dissension within its own ranks, financial constraints and difficulties over the dissemination and assessment of its projects. Beleaguered, badgered and branded by the DES as mediocre in performance, it certainly had no future in the face of the signals of centralism.

CHAPTER 10

BETTER SCHOOLS

The DES White Paper *Better Schools*

The North of England speech of January 1984 was finally translated into action with the publication in March 1985 of a DES White Paper under the title of *Better Schools*. This White Paper declared that the twin aims of the government were to raise the standard of schooling at all levels of ability and to secure the best possible return from the resources which were invested in education. The proposed measures to be taken by the government were wide ranging and classified under twelve principal headings. These were:

1. Curriculum
2. Examinations
3. Discipline
4. Truancy
5. Parents and schools
6. Teaching quality
7. Local education authority management
8. Minimum size of school
9. Education of ethnic minorities
10. The legal framework
11. Resources
12. The independent sector

Chapter 2 of the White Paper was devoted to the Primary and Secondary Curriculum and the section headed 'The Scope of Broadly Agreed Objectives' is especially worthy of attention.

'PURPOSES OF LEARNING AT SCHOOL'
Under this heading, a possible list was given as:

1. To help pupils to develop lively, enquiring minds, the ability to question and argue rationally and to apply themselves to tasks, and physical skills;

2. To help pupils to acquire understanding, knowledge and skills relevant to adult life and employment in a fast-changing world;

3. To help pupils to use language and numbers effectively;

4. To help pupils to develop personal moral values, respect for religious values, and tolerance of other races, religions, and ways of life;

5. To help pupils to understand the world in which they live, and the inter-dependence of individuals, groups and nations;

6. To help pupils to appreciate human achievements and aspirations.

BASIC PRINCIPLES

The Government maintained that such purposes required that the curriculum should reflect *a number of basic principles*:

1. The curriculum in both primary and secondary schools should be broad: as a whole and in its parts it should introduce the pupil to a wide range of areas of experience, knowledge and skill. The HMI surveys *Primary Education in England* and *Curriculum and Organisation of Primary Schools in Wales* both pointed conclusively to the fact that the teaching of language and mathematical skills in isolation or in a purely theoretical way was less effective than when they were associated with a wide-ranging programme of work which also included art and craft, history and geography, music, physical education, and science. This principle applies in respect of every pupil: it leaves no room for discrimination in the curriculum on grounds of sex;

2. The curriculum should be balanced: each area of the curriculum should be allotted sufficient time to make its specific contribution, but not so much that it squeezes out other essential areas;

3. The curriculum should be relevant: all subjects should be taught in such a way as to make plain their links with the pupils' own experience and to bring out their applications and continuing value in adult life. Related to this is the need for a practical dimension to learning, reflected both in the balance between subjects and in the content and teaching of subjects themselves. Most pupils take well to practical and other work which they believe will help them to get on in the modern world, whose technology they find stimulating rather than daunting. The curriculum should be devised and taught so as to harness such excitement and enthusiasm.

4. There should be careful differentiation: what is taught and how it is taught needs to be matched to pupils' abilities and aptitudes. It is of the greatest importance to stimulate and challenge all pupils, including the most and least able: within teaching groups as well as schools the range of ability is often wide.

AIMS OF THE PRIMARY CURRICULUM

As far as the primary phase was concerned the White Paper

declared that there was 'widespread agreement' that the curriculum should render it possible for this phase of education to:

1. Place substantial emphasis on achieving competence in the use of language (which, in Wales, may be Welsh as well as English, but which does not normally encompass foreign languages);

2. Place substantial emphasis on achieving competence in mathematics, in accordance with the recommendations of the Cockcroft Report;

3. Introduce pupils to science;

4. Lay the foundation of understanding in religious education, history and geography, and the nature and values of British society;

5. Introduce pupils to a range of activities in the arts;

6. Provide opportunities throughout the curriculum for craft and practical work leading up to some experience of design and technology and of solving problems;

7. Provide moral education, physical education and health education;

8. Introduce pupils to the nature and use in school and in society of new technology;

9. Give pupils some insights into the adult world, including how people earn their living.

'A CONTINUOUS AND COHERENT WHOLE'
On the question of the curriculum for the secondary phase of education, it was pointed out that:

> The 5–16 curriculum needs to be constructed and delivered as a continuous and coherent whole in which the primary phase prepares for the secondary phase and the latter builds on the former.

During the secondary period of schooling, it was stated that:

The Government believes that every pupil needs to continue in these years with English, mathematics, science and, save in exceptional circumstances, with physical education or games; should study elements drawn both from the humanities and the arts; and should take part in practical and technological work in a number of subjects, for example in CDT and not least in science. Most pupils should also continue with a foreign language. The place of religious education is governed by statute.

If programmes on these lines are to be pursued, it is likely that 80–85 per cent of each pupil's time needs to be devoted to subjects which are compulsory or liable to constrained choices and that only 15–20 per cent of that time can be left for studying subjects which are freely chosen and which supplement the compulsory and constrained part of the programme. Some schools already adopt this approach.

The compulsory and constrained elements ensure that each pupil's programme adequately prepares him for employment; they can support vocational aspirations which can then be further supported in the unconstrained elements of the programme. This approach is reflected in the evolving pattern of provision for 14–16 year olds within the TVEI, since the practical and technological aspects within TVEI courses are elements of a kind which should be in every pupil's programme. Free options provide an essential opportunity for enriching the curriculum with elements which appeal only to a minority of pupils, eg a further foreign language, or a particular aspect of the arts or applied subjects; they also make it possible to reinforce the compulsory and constrained part of the curriculum for less able pupils.

The need to secure breadth and balance in the limited study time available puts a premium on studies which maximise the opportunities for later learning. It is important that pre-vocational work and work experience designed to help pupils to prepare for employment should be kept broad and available to all pupils: and that courses designed to foster more specific vocational skills, popular though they may be with many pupils, should not displace courses of a more general character. The objective of the TVEI is to avoid these pitfalls in promoting, for the 14–18 age range, a variety of pre-vocational programmes which, during the first two years at least, form part of a broad and balanced curriculum.

The new technologies are exciting and challenging and can enrich the learning process in various ways; they will increasingly affect what pupils need to learn. Moreover, throughout the secondary phase room needs to be found for essential curricular elements which need not, or should not, be taught as separate subjects. For example some awareness of economic matters, notably the operation of market forces, the factors governing the creation of private and public wealth, and taxation, is a prerequisite for citizenship and employment; and health and sex education, taught within a moral framework, are a necessary preparation for responsible adulthood; whether they appear under these names in the timetable or are taught in connection with other courses or subjects is best left to the school's discretion. Other examples of such elements include careers education; personal and social education; moral education; and political education. On the other hand the issue of war and peace, for example, which naturally arises from many aspects of the curriculum should be treated in the context in which it arises; the Government believes that to assign a special place in the timetable to courses labelled 'peace studies' unbalances the curriculum and oversimplifies the issues involved.

Much of the curriculum argument in the *Better Schools* White Paper will be regarded as treading on by now familiar ground: it must be observed, however, that the overall stance of central government was becoming, perhaps ominously, increasingly definitive.

CHAPTER 11

THE CURRICULUM FROM 5–16

The DES White Paper *Better Schools* was paralleled in 1985 by a curriculum document from the Inspectorate under the title of *The Curriculum from 5–16*. (Curriculum Matters 2). To date, the 5–16 HMI curriculum document has proved to be the most practically useful of all the 'central' papers of the decade.

The paper did not aim to provide discussion and recommendations for each individual teaching subject and the subject label approach was presented in parallel publications in the Curriculum Matters Series (listed in Appendix 1).

The paper addressed itself to 'central professional issues' and it pulled together material from the primary, middle and secondary surveys along with conclusions which had emerged from the 11–16 'Red Book' series. It stressed the need for a unity of purpose throughout the 5–16 age span and criticised the often piecemeal nature of curriculum projects in individual curriculum areas.

It is important to note that the aim of the paper was to consider the questions which had been continually raised in the DES contributions, from the *professional* and classroom angle of teachers and their pupils. This approach rightly contrasted with what might be termed the *administrative* centralist approach of the DES itself.

The paper maintained that curriculum design and implementation should be viewed from two aspects. These were the *areas* of learning and the *elements* of learning.

The areas of learning

The definition of areas of learning coincided in most respects with the suggestions given repeatedly in earlier papers, with the important addition of technological experience as a necessary element in overall curriculum planning.

The sections covering these *areas* of learning, (originally the eight 'adjectives') gave examples of the kind of experience which would contribute to each given area. Thus in the development of aesthetic experience attention was drawn to the interrelated strands:

> One manifests itself through pupils creating their own works. . . the other comes from experiencing, interpreting or performing the works of other people, such as artists, composers, writers or architects. These two strands are mutually enriching and pupils need to interpret what they have heard, seen and felt at the same time as they try to express their own understandings and feelings in suitable media.

National curriculum debate continues to lay emphasis upon the 'basic' core subjects and upon testable elements, especially in the fields of mathematics, science and language. But it is essential that the wider aspects of the study of these subjects should remain in the forefront both of educational thinking and of classroom practice.

The sections of the 5–16 document which cover these areas of learning and experience are therefore given in detail as follows:

LINGUISTIC AND LITERARY
In this area of experience it was stated that:

This area is concerned with increasing pupils' command of language in listening, speaking, reading and writing. In part this will be achieved through the use of language for a variety of purposes in home and school, in part through the specific study of language and literature.

In order to work effectively, primary teachers should build on the language experience and skills which children possess on entry to school. It is, perhaps, insufficiently recognised that secondary teachers should begin with a similar understanding of their pupils' varied competences on entry to the secondary phase. All schools should provide a variety of contexts in which pupils may learn to respond to and use language for a variety of purposes. Language is generated and extended through the interaction of listening, speaking, reading, writing and experience. For example, young children who have made models in clay or who have listened to a story which has moved and informed them, are usually eager to talk about the experience. In doing so they clarify and extend both their thinking and their language, which assists them in their writing.

Through listening and talking in groups children are enabled to explore other people's experiences and to modify and extend their own.

This mutually reinforcing process deepens the understanding of the experience itself and prompts the development of their language. All pupils need to be given ample opportunity for discussion of a wide range of experiences encountered inside and outside school. The narration of their diaries by infants to their teacher can give practice in the ordering and sharing of information and feelings. Investigations in science can promote accurate description from direct observation, awareness of similarities and differences and speculation about cause and effect. Such activities provide opportunities for the teacher to sharpen the focus, extend the comment and prompt further speculation. Faced with such challenges children often need, not only to draw on their resources of vocabulary and familiar forms of expression, but also to try out new ways of expressing the meaning they want to convey. It is at this point, when there is a context of shared experience and an urgent need to communicate that the teacher's help can be most effective.

A range of language skills and competences needs to be developed throughout the years of schooling and across all subjects. Pupils should learn to speak with confidence, clarity and fluency, using forms of speech appropriate for a variety of audiences, involving a variety of situations and groupings and for a range of purposes of increasing complexity and demand. As they progress through the early stages of reading they should learn to read fluently, and with understanding , a range of different kinds of material, using methods appropriate to the material and the purposes for which they are reading; to have confidence in their capacities as readers; to enjoy reading for entertainment, for interest and for information; and to appreciate the necessity of reading for learning in most areas of the curriculum and for their personal lives. The pupils should write for a range of purposes; organise the content in ways appropriate to the purposes; use styles of writing appropriate to them and to the intended readership; and use spelling, punctuation and syntax accurately and with confidence. Pupils need to achieve a working knowledge of language so that they have a vocabulary for discussing it and are able to use it with greater awareness and control. That which characterises the achievement of older pupils is not only the accumulation of new knowledge or skills, but an increased ability to use language with sensitivity, sophistication and discrimination and to deal with more demanding forms of spoken and written language used by others.

Language is used in all areas of the 5 to 16 curriculum; it is the means of clarifying and of communicating the ideas which define relationships and establish patterns of working. Usually its form and vocabulary are similar to most subjects. Less commonly, it is used in a subject-specific sense where vocabulary carries a different meaning or emphasis from common usage, and where forms may take on a specialised character. Pupils should be encouraged to explore ideas which are new to them in their own words before being introduced to the technical terms for those ideas. Teachers in all subjects need to be proficient users of language themselves and to be aware of the difficulties which pupils may encounter when faced with new concepts expressed in technical vocabulary.

Works of literature, including those of other countries and of the ancient world, portray every aspect of human experience and bring that experience into sharp focus by refining both thought and language. The reading of literature, as well as being valuable in its own right, is, therefore, an essential part of the experience of language at all ages; it can extend pupils' understanding and sympathies and has a part to play in developing judgement. It can also illuminate many areas of the curriculum by the vividness and directness with which it can provide new experiences for some pupils and extend the experiences of others. Subjects such as history already use literary sources freely and many others could do so with advantage.

SCIENTIFIC

An understanding of the natural world and the world as modified by human beings was regarded as being within the province of the *scientific* area of learning and experience. In addition, scientific experience entailed the acquisition by pupils of the skills and competences which form the basis of scientific enquiry:

The scientific area of learning and experience is concerned with increasing pupils' knowledge and understanding of the natural world and the world as modified by human beings, and with developing skills and competences associated with science as a process of enquiry. These include observing, selecting from the observations whatever is important, framing hypotheses, devising and conducting experiments, communicating in oral and symbolic forms and applying the knowledge and understanding gained to new situations.

Pupils need to be taught to organise the data gathered through observation and investigation conducted by themselves and others. They should look for relationships or patterns and try to explain them. They should be encouraged to seek alternative explanations, to select those which seem most probable and to test them by experiments. Thus infants who notice that plants on a sunny window need watering more often than those in other parts of the classroom may be led to an investigation both into the evaporation of water and the rate at which water is taken up by plants. Such an investigation might involve the observation of what happens to water left in saucers in various parts of the school, considerations of plants of different sizes, noting temperature differences and the effect of ventilation. With young children, fine measurement might well be inappropriate: for example, it would probably suffice to distinguish between fairly crude categories in describing temperature. In due course, children are likely themselves to discover the need to make their observations progressively more exact.

The emphasis should be on considering real problems. Pupils should be encouraged to handle objects, to observe phenomena, to talk about these and to take part in enquiries through which skills related to science as a process can be developed. Careful observation using all the senses, with due regard to safety, should be encouraged, so that pupils become used to looking for differences and similarities in all kinds of contexts and to seeking explanations for them. Younger children might, for example compare the feeding habits of a hamster with those of a gerbil, or objects which sink with those which float. In the second example, some children will quickly notice that some objects float higher in the water or sink more quickly than others, and they should be encouraged to follow up their observation. An ecological study or the effects of heat and water on chemical elements can be the starting points for investigations with older pupils. It is not realistic to suppose that every single opportunity can be taken to turn a question into a practical investigation, but making the most of such opportunities should lie at the heart of science teaching and learning.

MATHEMATICAL

In *mathematical* experience it was stressed that for some children competence in this area would become a particularly important acquisition:

For some pupils competence in mathematics will become a particularly important acquisition, either in its own right, or because of its application in science, engineering and many other branches of learning. But all pupils need to learn a variety of mathematical concepts and processes if they are to understand and appreciate relationships and pattern in both number and space in their everyday lives and be able to express them clearly and concisely.

Mathematics is taught to virtually all pupils for the whole period of compulsory schooling. Many children in primary schools find enjoyment and excitement in mathematical work, whether it occurs within the lessons devoted to the subject, or elsewhere in the curriculum, especially when it is varied and applied to real situations. At best, they learn that mathematical ideas can be talked about and experimented with, and that they can be used along with other ideas to solve a problem, or express a point of view. As pupils proceed through the secondary school, there is too often a tendency for mathematical procedures to be taught at the expense of pupils' involvement and understanding, with the result that many find the subject increasingly difficult and unappealing. It is always important to explore a problem in familiar terms in order to decide upon, and understand the working of, a particular mathematical process.

Although mathematics might be regarded as the most abstract of subjects, it was pointed out that:

It should often arise from, and give rise to, extensive practical activity and investigation. The range of mathematical experience to which pupils are exposed ought therefore to be as broad as possible. Young children should be introduced to mathematics through guided play with materials such as sand and water, and through shopping and domestic play. These can give experience in a range of mathematical topics including capacity and money, and provide opportunities for discrimination, classification and quantitative description. As children get older their needs and interests change but there is still a fundamental need, throughout their schooling, for their mathematical development to be grounded in relevant, practical experiences. There is strong evidence to suggest that, where there is this emphasis, mastery of the so-called basic skills is more likely to occur than when there is a narrow concentration on the skills themselves.

All pupils need to be encouraged to respond orally and to discuss their work. This will help them to clarify their own thoughts, to tackle real life problems which are drawn from a variety of experiences in and out of school and to carry out mathematical investigations. In addition it will help the teacher to assess their level of understanding. Development of pupils' capacity for reasoning, including logical deduction, should be encouraged, for example, in connection with everyday things and activities encountered in the classroom, at home or out of doors.

Mathematical concepts and processes involving, for example, number, order, weight, length, time, money, computation and formulae receive attention in mathematics lessons. The mathematical area is much broader than this, however, and is dealt with not only in the teaching of the subject itself but also in other activities and subjects of the curriculum. It is to be found, for example, in topic work, art, science, home economics, craft and geography, where the mathematical experience may include the construction of geometrical designs, making graphs, costing, estimating and measuring in planning a meal, quantifying results and using grid references. Older pupils should see that in all kinds of speech and writing mathematical concepts are present, sometimes in linguistic forms such as analogy or in considerations of magnitude and spatial relationships. Mathematical experiences are also linked with aesthetic experiences, for example in the consideration of the proportions of a building, or the physical balance of the gymnast.

The elements of learning

The *elements* of learning were defined under the headings of:

- *Knowledge* (in the sense of factual content).
- *Skill acquisition* (subdivided into communication, observation, study, problem solving, physical and practical, creative and imaginative, numerical, and social and personal).
- *Attitudes*.

These elements of learning were intended to act as a complementary check list to the areas of learning sections. The concepts of areas of learning and elements of learning are complementary since each subject area is likely to provide, to a varying degree, elements of factual knowledge, elements of skill acquisition and elements which go towards the formation of attitudes.

Additionally the paper proposed a set of 'characteristics' which were regarded as essential if opportunities for all pupils to engage in a *national and comparable range of learning* were to be realised. These characteristics were enumerated as:

1. Breadth
2. Balance
3. Relevance
4. Differentiation
5. Progression and continuity

To ensure breadth any overall curriculum must ensure that each area of experience is represented in the total timetable of individual pupils. The curriculum plan must aim for a balance between the areas of experience, expressed in subject terms. It must take care that the curriculum context is relevant to all pupils and is not enmeshed with 'clutter'. It must allow for differentiation in accordance with the talents and abilities of each pupil. Finally, it must cater for progression in pupils' learning and avoid repetitive or static situations. This progression and continuity of approach in learning must occur both inside the school and between the schools which make up 'the stages' of the schooling process.

The significance, therefore, of the 5–16 curriculum document lies in its contributions in the field of syllabus building, whole school coherent curriculum policy and, perhaps most importantly, in its aide-memoire capacity for 'justificatory' procedures in the preparation of subject schemes of work.

PUPIL ASSESSMENT
With prescience, the 5–16 curriculum paper concluded with an important section on pupil assessment.

Assessment is inseparable from the teaching process since its prime purpose is to improve pupils' performance. It should help teachers to diagnose pupils' strengths and weaknesses; to match the work of the classroom to their capabilities; to guide them into appropriate courses and groups; to involve them in discussion and self-appraisal; and, in reports and all meetings, to inform their parents of progress. A second purpose is to enable the teachers to see how far their objectives are being met and to adjust them and their teaching approaches accordingly. This is best done by reviewing pupils' progress in the light of what the teachers have set out to do.

If schools are to fulfil these aims of assessment, development is needed in three main areas: clearer definition of expectations as expressed through the aims and objectives of curricula and schemes of work; improved methods of assessment in the classroom on a day-to-day basis; and improved methods of recording and reporting progress.

Improvement in performance must be measured against a clear identification of what it is hoped pupils will experience, learn and master. This in turn requires that aims and objectives be known and expressed in schemes of work which set out the content, concepts, skills and attitudes to be acquired and the teaching approaches and learning resources to be used. It follows that pupils need to be given tasks which allow them to demonstrate their competence across the range of performance expected of them. In this sense the assessment process is an integral part of the curriculum. Not all schools have such detailed schemes of work and, where they do, assessment and recording are seldom based on the detailed expectations set out in them.

Assessment involves a mixture of techniques, many of them subjective, which the teacher learns with experience to apply to day-to-day observation of how pupils perform across the range of tasks, including discussion and questioning, and to the scrutiny of written work. While few teachers articulate fully the measures which they use, or the yardsticks which they apply to performance, these forms of assessment have the virtue of being an integral part of classroom activity. A range of techniques should be used to suit the purpose and the activity.

The Assessment of Performance Unit has conducted surveys of mathematics, English, foreign languages and science to discover how pupils of all abilities approach and perform tasks in these subjects. It has described frameworks for assessment and how to use them and has developed many new techniques of assessment, some of which are capable of adaptation for use by teachers in their schools. Work is also in hand to suggest teaching strategies which will enable pupils to avoid many common errors and misconceptions.

Much of the assessment described above has to go on in the busy environment of the classroom and must be largely impressionistic, though teachers need additional time to record their impressions. From time to time also, informal assessment needs to be supported by more objective forms of testing, such as class tests and examinations devised by the teacher, which should be closely related to the work in hand. Similarly, graded assessments, which have become common in recent years, should reflect the full range of classroom activities. Care must be taken to see that tests do not dominate the work and that they do not so itemise the work that coherence is lost. Occasional use needs to be made also of standardised tests, particularly tests of reading and numeracy, to help in establishing a base line of performance, for screening purposes, or for the diagnosis of particular difficulties. While these tests have the advantage of greater objectivity, they can too easily be divorced from classroom work and their use should therefore be limited.

Recording and reporting progress are the most helpful if the findings can be used by others, as well as teachers and pupils, to illuminate current strength and weaknesses and show specific ways of improving performance. Often, however, characteristics of performance are merged into a series of global marks or grades which are of little use as a guide to future learning needs. Because the record is 'general' the report, designed to inform parents and others, is often similarly unhelpful. 'Could do better' provides no indication of which specific aspects of the work need improvement. Good practice does exist, however, and it is invariably related to specification by the teacher of clear learning targets and discussion of them with individual pupils. In this way pupils do not need to wait for a report to learn how they are progressing. The learning targets and progress towards achieving them are shared between teacher and pupil.

The final sentences on assessment deserve reiteration:

> *Pupils do not need to wait for a report to learn how they are progressing. The learning targets and progress towards achieving them are shared between teacher and pupil.*

CHAPTER 12

THE RESPONSE OF THE LEAs

From the start of the curriculum debate, passing references had been made to the role of the local authorities and their responsibilities with regard to the curriculum in their schools. In the 1944 Act the role of the LEAs and likewise the responsibilities of the DES had in curriculum terms been defined very loosely.

It was not until the late 1970s that the central searchlight came to be increasingly focused upon the 'providers' of education in the 104 counties and boroughs of England and Wales. Although each authority employed its own advisers or inspectors as part of their total professional staff, the size, quality and the responsibility of the local education authority advisory service varied immensely. LEA advisers frequently had to undertake administrative duties, play a part in the appointment of school staffs, and supervise probationary teachers.

With some exceptions the role of the local authorities therefore in the national curriculum planning stakes had remained persistently shadowy.

The School Curriculum

In 1983, however, the DES issued a Circular (No 8/83) under the heading of *The School Curriculum*. The circular called for:

1. A report on the progress which has been made in drawing up policies for the curriculum in primary and secondary schools.

2. Details of the involvement of teachers, governors, parents and the local community in drawing up the policy.

3. A description of the ways in which the policy is being given practical effect in the schools.

4. Details of the steps taken to ensure that the curriculum is balanced,

coherent, suited to pupils across the full range of ability, related to what happens outside schools and that it includes sufficient applied and practical work.

5. Details of the effect of the availability of resources on putting curriculum policies into practice.

Local Authority Policies for the School Curriculum

Although all LEAs were asked to provide their replies by April of the following year, it was three years before the DES was able to issue a summarised response to the circular. The analysis of the replies appeared in June 1986, entitled *Local Authority Policies for the School Curriculum*. Because of the passage of time the DES summary was now able to refer in its opening paragraphs to the Government's 1985 White Paper *Better Schools*, where it had been stated that the Government's twin goals were to raise the standard achieved by pupils and to secure the best possible return for the resources devoted to the schools.

It was pointed out in the review that the LEA responses reflected the nature of the original circular, which dealt mainly with *The Processes within Authorities for preparing and giving effect to their Curricular Policies*. The 1983 circular had not considered in detail the *substance* of LEA policies on the curriculum, and these important aspects therefore did not surface in the DES review paper.

Nevertheless, the final paragraphs (60–63) of the review were aimed at edging forward the Government's view that there was an urgent need for detailed curricular policy statements:

As authorities themselves recognise, there is still much to be done to give their policies practical effect. The LEAs are at very different stages in this process, but the picture which emerges is of much progress at every level of the education service, involving governing bodies and sometimes parents as well as advisers, heads and staffs of schools.

While there is now little dissent about the need for curricular policies at LEA and school level and about some of the principles on which those policies should be based, the degree of common understanding about the way to put such principles into effect varies. Areas which stand out as meriting further attention in this respect include: the need for greater differentiation within the curriculum to meet the needs of each pupil, recognising that a wide range of ability and aptitude will be present in most teaching groups; the need for teaching approaches to reflect the curricular aims and objectives which have been formulated; and the need for practical steps to achieve real continuity between the primary and secondary phases, including continuity both in the curriculum and in teaching approaches.

The most important sentence in the review document was left until the last:

> *Progress in defining and applying nationally agreed objectives can only be made as a joint activity involving all the partners in the education service and the clients they serve.*

CHAPTER 13

THE 1986 ACT

The new 'scaffolding' of the educational process as foreshadowed by Sir Keith Joseph in 1984 and schematised in the *Better Schools* White Paper of March 1985, became statutory with the passing of the 1986 Education Act. This Act received Royal Assent in November 1986 and its principal provisions related to the role of the LEA and the place of governors and parents as consumers and guardians of education at local level.

Sections 17 and 18 of the act are of special importance in relation to the curriculum. Thus:

Section 17 makes it a duty of the LEA to make and keep up to date a written statement of its policy in relation to the secular curriculum, copies of which will be available for inspection in schools.

Section 18 makes it a duty of the governing body of a county, controlled or maintained special school to consider the LEA's policy (with regard to matters other than sex education) for the secular curriculum; what should be the general aims of the secular curriculum for the school; and how, if at all in their opinion, the LEA's statement should be modified for their school. The governing body will have to consult the head teacher and also the LEA when considering these matters. They will also have to give a copy of their statement to the LEA and head teacher, and it will be available for inspection at the school. The governing body will be required to review their aims for the curriculum if a school's circumstances change.

The governing body will have to consider separately, while having regard to the LEA's statement under Section 17 of the Act, whether sex education should form part of the curriculum of the school. They will have a duty to maintain a written statement of how sex education should be taught, and to set down any decision they may make for it not to form part of the curriculum. Again, the statement will be available for inspection at the school.

The head teacher will be responsible for determining and organising the curriculum within the school in a way that is compatible with the policy of the LEA, or if incompatible with that policy, with that policy as modified by the governing body. So far as sex education is concerned, the head teacher will have to ensure that the curriculum is compatible with the governing body's policy, provided that this does not conflict with the syllabus of any public examination.

Any persons connected with the community served by the school or the relevant chief officer of police may make representations to the governing body and head teacher about the curriculum which they will be required to consider.

The basic composition of the governing body which would be required to consider these 'representations' was laid down in Section 3 of the Act as follows:

Pupil numbers	Parents	LEA	Headteacher	Teacher	Co-opted (or, for controlled schools: foundation/ co-opted)	Total
up to 99	2	2	1	1	3 (2/1)	9
100–299	3	3	1	1	4 (3/1)	12
300–599	4	4	1	2	5 (4/1)	16
600 or more	5	5	1	2	6 (4/2)	19

Many of the remaining sections of the Act dealt with contingent matters, such as the position of voluntary schools, procedures for exclusion from school, the right of appeal by parents etc. For the sake of completeness a summary of the Act is reproduced in Appendix 2.

CORPORAL PUNISHMENT IN SCHOOLS

Section 47 of the Act is of historic importance. Dealing with the question of corporal punishment in schools, it provided for its abolition in maintained schools, non-maintained special schools and voluntary aided schools. It also dealt with cases of children who receive education 'otherwise than at school', and it covered children who hold assisted place status in independent schools.

CHAPTER 14

RESOURCES AND THE CURRICULUM

It is a truism that good resources do not ensure good schools. Nevertheless there is a basic and undeniable link between levels of resources and levels of achievement in the educational system.

In 1976, HM Inspectors, as part of their routine visiting programme, began to collect evidence on the observed effects of local authority expenditure policies on educational provision in England. Their findings were summarised in an annual report and these reports become public from 1984.

Report by HMI on the effects of local authority expenditure policies on education provision in England – 1985

The principal findings of the 1985 report illustrate the connections between levels of resource provision and the quality of education in the maintained sector of education:

These principal findings attempt to identify and articulate important messages for the education service about levels of resources for education and the quality of what it does. Such links between resources and quality are not straightforward, and those familiar adversaries of clarity and simplicity, (shifting numbers of pupils and extensive variations in provision and practice), confuse an already complicated picture. During the past year the disturbing influences of these factors were augmented by the obvious and not so obvious effects of the teachers' pay dispute that affected LEAs, schools, teachers and pupils variously throughout the period of our survey.

As in recent years there has been *little overall change in the total resource provision made for education by the large majority of LEAs.* In secondary schools there were some further improvements in pupil - teacher ratios (PTRs), while in many primary schools some of the previously unplanned improvements in PTRs have been reversed as school rolls rise. There have also been continuing improvements in the number of advisers and advisory teachers, in the provision for in-service education and training (INSET) and in the supply of consumable materials. The slightly improved provision for books, noted last year, has not been repeated and provision has only been held steady this last year, while that for equipment and furniture has deteriorated. . .

Small improvements in the provision for schools have sometimes been made but do not apply consistently either across or within LEAs, primary and secondary phases, or institutions. Disparities in provision within and between schools, and in turn the opportunities available to pupils, are widening as a result of various factors: these include local policy decisions; further increases in the financial contributions made by parents and others to some schools; and central government initiatives such as introduction of the Technical and Vocational Education Initiative (TVEI), the lower attaining pupils project (LAPP) and the Education Support Grants (ESGs). Furthermore, where low baselines of provision have now been operating for some years in some LEAs, increases of the sort noted are not sufficient to enable all schools to respond confidently and effectively to the many calls for change and development aimed at improving the overall levels of achievement of pupils.

Throughout the system *the large majority of the work seen was judged satisfactory or better*, though the actual proportion in schools was slightly lower than that in the previous two years. Variations in the proportion of work judged satisfactory were evident for different schools, for different age groups, and for pupils of different ability levels. In all schools it was the work of pupils of below average ability which was least satisfactory. In many lessons teachers were failing to differentiate adequately between their pupils on the basis of sound judgements of pupil potential and their educational needs. Taking all institutions together the most frequently noted factor affecting the work was again the quality of teaching. This was followed, in order, by the identification of pupils' and students' needs, the match between the teachers' qualifications and experience and the work being undertaken, the level, deployment and management of resources, and the pupils' behaviour. Though the relationship between the quality of work and levels of resources is acknowledged to be complex and direct causal links impossible to make, the data and its analysis confirmed that *there is a statistically significant association between satisfactory or better levels of appropriate resources and work of sound quality, and between unsatisfactory levels of resources and poor quality work.*

The quality of the leadership and management offered by subject co-ordinators, heads of department, heads, principals and LEAs made a vital contribution not only to the quality of present work of pupils and students but also to the capacity of institutions to bring about change and improvement in order to raise standards of achievements. In over a quarter of the schools visited poor leadership and management at one or more levels was considered to be adversely affecting the quality of work, the levels and deployment of resources, the organisation and planning of the curriculum, the take-up of INSET, the behaviour of pupils, and the morale of teachers. In only half the schools visited was the planning and organisation of the pupils' work, including relating tasks carefully to the age, ability and aptitude of the pupils, judged satisfactory. Better planning of some of the work, and the necessary time to do it, with all that that means for the organisation and management of the institutions, was required in about one-third of the schools visited. Over the last three years this same picture has emerged with little sign of any significant improvement. . . .

There is evidence that in an increasing proportion of LEAs more attention is being paid to the management of aspects of the education service. More LEAs are developing and implementing explicit and systematic policies in relation to the curriculum and staffing; the role and function of the inspectorate; and the matching of INSET provision to the identified needs of the service, schools and individual teachers. In some cases this is the result of centrally provided resources being targeted on specific developments. These improvements in LEA management need to continue and become more widespread if the system as a whole is to derive the maximum possible benefits from the finite resources available to education.

While the overall number of teachers has decreased, though proportionately more slowly than the number of pupils, this year has seen an increase in the number of pupils and teachers in primary schools. While generally the number of teachers is adequate for the work currently being undertaken there is evidence of *increasing shortages of sufficient teachers in subjects such as mathematics, physical science and CDT, and for early years education.* The establishment and maintenance of a broad, balanced curriculum for every pupil remains a problem, partly because relatively few LEAs in practice are implementing a policy of allocating teachers to schools in order to staff an agreed curriculum; partly because of the wide range and variation in PTRs both between and within LEAs; and partly because a substantial number of teachers are not placed where their expertise and experience are most needed. The consequence of this is that there is a mismatch between the initial qualifications and experience of some teachers and their teaching programmes; some curricular experiences are no longer available to all pupils; and some schools seek to maintain some subject work by teaching during lunch time or after school. Systematic attention to coherent INSET policies related to identified teacher and curricular development needs would contribute to solving the difficulties, but in addition there is a need for the carefully planned and sensitively executed redeployment of some teachers . . . .

The steady improvements made each year since 1981 in the provision of books for schools was not continued in the last year although provision was held steady. There are many schools with insufficient numbers of books; others with old stock which cannot be replaced; and many which are having to choose between the replacement of old stock and the purchase of the books needed to introduce new courses and examinations. Both schools and FHE face the continuing difficulty of replacing ageing capital items of equipment, particularly in practical subjects or where technological change is most rapid. The problem is much more acute in schools than in FHE but in the longer term less complex, demanding and costly. However, the picture is patchy, caused in part by the continuing wide variations in the capitation made available to schools; the growing differences in parental contributions to schools; and the funding made available through specific national curriculum development projects such as the TVEI, ESGs and the LAP projects.

It is clear that the disparities in provision both between and within LEAs and institutions are increasing. The variations in PTRs, capitation, parental contributions, and the selectivity of funding deriving from schemes such as the TVEI and the ESGs, all contribute in various ways to the differences in provision observed for similar pupils and for those of different ages and ability groups. In general, in terms of levels of resources, the 11–16 age group is less well provided for than are the 16–19 year olds, while the 16–19 year olds are better provided for in NAFE than in schools. . . .

The condition of much of the accommodation used by pupils, students, teachers and lecturers continues to deteriorate. Last year's report warned that without urgent attention the cost of putting things right would become prohibitive. There has been no such improvement. In fact there has been no improvement overall in the state of school buildings since 1981, and the current programmes of maintenance in many LEAs suggest that the situation is likely to continue to worsen. The quality of the furniture available is also now becoming of concern as schools find it increasingly difficult to replace worn, inappropriate items. In some schools and colleges the conditions in which teaching and learning take place adversely affect the quality of pupils' and students' work and do nothing to encourage their sense of enjoyment and pride in their school or college. In many more the environment is shabby and uninviting and does little to stimulate learning or to impress parents or other visitors. The cost of attending to these problems, added to those arising in some authorities from vandalism and arson, is mounting and has now reached proportions where it is difficult to see how on present funding the education service can prevent further decline let alone reverse the situation . . .

It is the schools sector where there is cause for most concern. It is getting by and providing satisfactorily for most pupils in many places by robbing Peter to pay Paul; doing less; or with the help of sizeable contributions from parents. There are sharp polarisations in provision between schools in different parts of the country and within the same LEA. Where hard decisions about priorities have to be made at LEA level it tends to be building maintenance, redecoration and furniture replacement programmes that suffer. At school level it is the least able in all types of school and top junior and early year secondary pupils who appear to bear the brunt of reduced or inappropriate provision. In addition many schools are finding it increasingly difficult to replace old books, equipment and furniture; to implement curricular change; and to respond to planned changes in assessment and examination procedures.

Not all these problems are directly or indirectly attributable to absolute shortages of money and resources and it is clear that more of either or both would not solve all the difficulties. *There is a marked need for efficient and effective management of people and resources at every level of the service*; improved leadership; INSET better matched to the identified needs of teachers, schools and colleges; and, above all, much clearer perceptions by teachers of pupils' potential and needs, and an improved differentiation of the tasks set so as to better match the pupils' ages, aptitudes and abilities. But addressing any or all of these has a cost in money, time or both and to be effective that cost will not be cheap.

As always it is high quality teaching that is at the heart of good education. Such teaching is present throughout the system but is not as general or widespread as any concerned party would wish. For that which exists to be sustained, and for more of it to be spread more generally throughout schools and colleges, there is a need for the resources necessary to do the job well; decent, stimulating conditions in which to work; and that respect and support which are the mirror images of professional commitment and competence. This report shows that most teaching and learning are satisfactory or better; that there is not numerically a shortage of teachers; and that most schools are not falling down, leaking or facing crises in the availability of materials and equipment. That many schools are being affected in these ways, and many teachers and pupils working in depressing conditions with inadequate resources, support and leadership, is adversely affecting much of what goes on in our schools. Few involved in providing or providing for education can take much, if any, pride in a national service within which three-tenths of all the lessons seen were unsatisfactory; one-fifth was adversely affected by poor accommodation; a quarter was suffering from shortages of equipment; *in three-fifths of the schools where an assessment was possible, the teachers' perceptions of pupils' potential and needs were inadequate; and half the schools visited needed to widen their range of teaching styles to bring about a better match with what was being taught if the changes and improvements called for by national policies for education were to be achieved.* The damaging effects of all this on pupil performance and on the teachers' morale and their ability and willingness to bring about much needed change are showing themselves clearly.

All that needs to be done has a cost, and everything cannot be done at once. But given agreement about priorities, sufficient and suitably targeted resources, effectively and efficiently managed, the education service should be capable of developing the better trained, equipped, well-led and managed teaching force needed to raise standards generally to the levels currently achieved by the best schools and intended by so many national and local policies for raising the standards of pupil and student achievement.

Implications

The implications of expenditure policies on the school curriculum were summarised in the final section of the report on overall provision:

While most LEAs appear to have maintained their overall levels of provision for schools, the baselines which have been established for some of that provision are insufficient to provide the resources necessary for them and their schools to respond successfully to national and local calls for improvements in pupils' achievements and in curriculum planning and development.[1]

1. The 1985 Report was the last to appear in what had come to be regarded as the 'traditional' format. The 1986 Report (published in July 1987) differed in focus from previous reports and presented underlying data in tabulated form. However, as the section on 'principal messages' declared: *'In broad terms, the picture given by this report is not significantly changed from that of 1985'.*

CHAPTER 15

MICROELECTRONICS AND THE CURRICULUM

The Microelectronics Programme

One of the success stories in curriculum innovation at methodology level emerged with the advent of *The Microelectronics Programme* (MEP). Sponsored at governmental level in 1981, it was stated that:

> The aim of the Programme is to help schools to prepare children for life in a society in which devices and systems based on microelectronics are commonplace and pervasive . . .
>
> In developing a strategy for the Programme it has been assumed that:

(i) schools should be encouraged to respond to these changes by amending the content and approach of individual subjects in the curriculum and, in some cases, by developing new topics;

(ii) with the dual aim of enriching the study of individual subjects and of familiarising pupils with the use of the microcomputer itself, methods of teaching and learning should make use of the microcomputer and other equipment using microprocessors. This may be expected to add new and rewarding dimensions to the relationship between teacher and class or teacher and pupil;

(iii) use should be made of the microcomputer to develop the individual pupil's capacity for independent learning and information retrieval;

(iv) for those children with physical handicaps, new devices should be used to help them to adjust to their environment while those with mental handicaps should be encouraged and supported by computer programs and other learning systems which make use of new technologies.

The project came to an end in 1986, and even discounting the 'Hawthorne effect' of the MEP, it is fair to say that very many school children now possess a 'hands on' awareness of computer aspects of living in a technological age. Much of this awareness has come from school, but of equal influence has been the 'école parallèle' of the outside world – the home, the media and the entertainment industry.

Subsequent situation

In school situations, microcomputers have still featured either as an electronic blackboard or been relegated to 'games' situations.

To enable teachers to stand back and evaluate the quality of their work with microcomputers, and to enable an assessment of long-term achievements to be made for future 'feedback', a number of questions must be considered:

1. It is necessary to reflect upon the impact of the use of microcomputers on the *learning styles of the pupils* – has the use of the microcomputer in fact replaced an existing style of learning, e.g. a didactic lesson, or a group discussion? Has it added to the opportunities for individualised learning?

2. Consideration should be given to the question of the impact upon the children's *skill acquisition* – apart from the familiarisation skill, has there been any effect, e.g. upon the learning time and the quality of the children's number skill acquisition, their communication skills and their problem solving skills?

3. Most importantly, has the microcomputer element in teaching programmes significantly added to children's *knowledge and understanding* in ways which were not so readily and rapidly achievable by 'traditional' teaching methods?

HMI 1987 report on the Programme

The HMI report of 1987 on the Microelectronics Programme attempted an assessment of these features, with examples at primary and secondary level as follows:

Learning styles – secondary schools

There was evidence that, with experience, the use of microelectronic devices in the classroom changed teaching and learning styles. There were many examples where computer programs were used as an electronic blackboard calling for only passive involvement by pupils, or of pupils using programs that required only repetitious practice of simple techniques. At the same time there was some evidence that, with greater familiarity with computer based learning, teachers tended to abandon these types of program in favour of more open-ended materials which encouraged pupils to speculate and to explore ideas. By the end of the survey there was a greater incidence of this use of software. MEP staff and LEA advisers felt that the time taken for these newer approaches to be accepted in schools was often underestimated. For example, in mathematics, 'drill and practice' programs were often seen in use during the early stages of the survey. The novelty of initial computer use meant that pupils clearly enjoyed the repetitive exercises with immediate feedback from the program, allowing the activity to continue with minimum teacher intervention. Experience with IT and clearly targeted in-service courses were needed before many teachers moved to more challenging programs. In home economics the most successful IT-related work was seen in departments which were already engaged in active curriculum development and where exploratory work and planning in the context of home making were already commonplace in lessons. Where the MFA materials were used it was usual to see teachers adopt an approach that encouraged pupils to explore problems for themselves.

While some of the changes noted in learning styles can be attributed to the use of MEP products on their own, where INSET was closely involved with the introduction of new materials there was a greater likelihood of change. There were examples of pupils teaching themselves to use programs, particularly where independent learning styles were already adopted. Packages like NEWSROOM encouraged the development of many worthwhile skills, requiring co-operative group work and the evaluation of evidence, for example. (This is a package which allows the computer and printer to simulate a teleprinter using 'newsflashes' created by the teacher in the context of an imaginary or real incident. Pupils have to assess and combine the various items into a news story, for newspaper, radio, teletext or television.) Where computers were used in music it became possible for pupils to experiment with composition and to listen to the outcomes of their efforts even though they had very limited skills of musical performance.

Classroom and resource management
In the early months of the MEP there were few microcomputers in schools and this constraint, in itself, imposed a particular style of working. The increased provision of machines gave much more flexibility, with individual, group and whole class use becoming possible. Imaginative teachers in various subjects could clearly turn even limited software to good use. There were also examples of good software and often materials being poorly used because of poor management of time or equipment. Some

teachers tried to provide practical work for a whole class by seating the entire class at a limited number of computers. In one case pupils were set to work in groups of six to a machine and this proved unsatisfactory, as many were clearly reduced to the role of observers. In another case, however, the limitation on the number of computers caused a teacher to organise a whole-class discussion around a single micro linked to a large monitor. The pupils were involved in discussing among themselves and with the teacher the information which was being entered into and requested from the micro. The pupils took turns in keying in the class decisions and requests. This was a difficult teaching situation but one which turned out to be successful in these particular circumstances.

In secondary schools, the acquisition of more computers did not necessarily lead to better use. Where, as so often was the case, all new equipment went into a computer room it was mainly used to support computer familiarisation and computer studies courses. Its influence in the school as a whole was then very slight. MEP identified this as a problem and attempted, by means of its INSET packages, courses and conferences, to encourage the use of IT in as many subject studies as possible. Despite this, many children came from primary schools with a reasonable degree of familiarity with computers, but had little opportunity to use this expertise and to develop the learning styles with IT which they had met in their primary schools.

In schools with pupils with special needs the more easily accessible the micro was within the classroom the more frequently it was used and the quicker was the teacher's appreciation of broader usage. It was significant that those schools which had several micros appeared to be more advanced in appraising their strategies of deployment than schools which had few machines. In schools with limited hardware the teachers often only used basic software which could be easily run and monitored. In both mainstream and special education even good materials could be misused. This happened where leadership and INSET in the use of IT were lacking. It also happened where teachers regarded work with computers as a reward for good behaviour, say, or as a discrete, unrelated time-filler in lessons rather than an integral part of planned learning and teaching.

Successful examples

The Microelectronics For All (MFA) course for secondary pupils was seen in a number of schools (by the end of the Programme one fifth of secondary schools in the country had a class set of this equipment). Pupils were frequently seen enthusiastically discussing the set tasks in small groups, suggesting and trying various solutions – they delighted in making things work. In one school it was noted that all the pupils involved were motivated to work hard for well over an hour. They displayed a sound understanding of the principles involved; could offer extended responses to questions; demonstrate a range of solutions, discuss their relative merits; and compare results. Similar skills were also noted with other microelectronics control technology equipment in a girls' school. However, although the associated teacher INSET materials stressed the importance of this problem solving approach and of applying the concepts to relevant industrial and domestic examples, a number of classes were observed to work through the material in a pedestrian way, preoccupied with routine writing tasks rather than the exploration of control techniques.

One MEP mathematics project was designed to develop short computer programs which could be written by pupils to support their own learning of mathematics. For instance, at one secondary school a fourth year mixed ability class was working in a computer base with two or three pupils to a terminal. They typed in a 10 line program that had been designed by the teacher which, when run, produced a geometrical pattern. By altering the various parameters pupils had to establish the connection with the changed geometrical shapes. Pupils of all abilities worked hard and profitably for the whole of a double period during which they were engaged in useful dialogue and investigation. At another school a similar strategy was adopted with a group of sixth form mathematicians who were engaged on a study of differential equations. Although the programming expertise of the pupils was limited they soon grasped the elementary coding and benefited greatly from new insights into the mathematics which this process and its results provided. Moreover, motivated by the computing facility and the teaching approach, these pupils were soon experimenting with ideas well beyond the starting points suggested by the teacher.

Learning styles – primary schools

The importance of experience
A relatively small number of the schools visited were 'experienced' users of computers, and the majority were within 12 to 18 months of receiving their machines. In numerous cases pupils were further advanced than their teachers in using the computer because of the growth in sales on the home market. Most of the examples of teachers' early attempts to use IT within their lessons followed a pattern of pupil familiarisation with the operation of the equipment and with individuals or small groups working through a program which the whole class would eventually complete. The software was often not relevant to other class work, though drill and practice programs related to mathematics or language activities were frequently popular and considered by staff as 'safe activities'.

The management of the computer, not only within the classroom but in the school as a whole, still had to be considered seriously by many schools. The MEP had an influence indirectly through its involvement at different levels of INSET and there was a number of publications in which the Programme gave advice through case studies. There was a clear indication that MEP's National Primary Project was firmly committed to encouraging the use of the computer as a support for good primary practice throughout the school, rather than as an object of study in itself.

IT and teaching style
Where teachers were confident in using both hardware and software, encouraging and exciting uses were identified. There was increasing

103

evidence of change in traditional styles of teaching and learning. For example, by using word-processors some children become more confident in their writing; similarly the gathering and sorting of complicated information was found to be within the scope of young primary age pupils. Both EDWORD and FACTFILE are examples of such MEP funded programs which were successfully used. Reference is made elsewhere in this report to these examples. When 6 or 7 year old children were seen using the MICROWRITER (or QUINKEY)*, as part of a MEP supported project, they typically persevered for over an hour on a writing task; were motivated to work in groups; began to use more punctuation than previously and showed more improvement in spelling. Likewise, when children were using computer adventure games there were many examples of good cooperative activity; extended concentration; and a greater willingness to explore ideas than might normally be expected. This good practice was usually seen where the class teacher was already an exponent of cooperative group work. There was also some evidence that good programs supported by good INSET encouraged teachers to venture into, what was for them, a new style of working.

Skills – secondary schools

Communication skills

Communication skills – both literary and oral – were often increased as a result of discussion and small group work fostered by some CBL programs. The best of these required pupils to work in groups, often referring to other information sources. Adventure games were useful in this context and some database problems were seen being thoughtfully discussed by less able pupils. However, this sort of activity was less frequently noted in secondary than in primary schools. Where schools were beginning to use wordprocessing there was evidence of children writing more – one boy who had previously never written more than 40 words constructed a 400 word story – and, more importantly, to a higher standard than previously. The program NEWSROOM encouraged a whole range of communication skills. During one lesson, organised for a year group of 11 year olds, the community policeman and another non-teacher adult were involved to provide reality and interviewing experience. The pupils discussed the newsflashes as they appeared; assessed the validity of the source before deciding on head-lines; and composed the 'story'. They were highly motivated, most showed sustained concentration and much of the language work was of good quality.

* The MICROWRITER is a small handheld text generator with only six keys, used in place of the QWERTY keyboard. A subsequent and much cheaper development for educational use has been the QUINKEY keyboard, which can only be used with a computer and VDU. It is sold in sets of four which are linked to a single micro. Typically, children work in groups of four at a time using one keyboard each.

Observational skills

Observational, deductive and predictive skills were often improved where pupils were using database programs to record and analyse observations – in environmental studies and some science lessons for example. In one school the information gained from a field study trip was classified and entered as a file in a database program. Pupils then searched for patterns and relationships using the program to test hypotheses.

Study skills

Few teachers realised the extent to which pupils could improve their study through using the computer. Material for handling information was produced by the CAIS domain for use by both teachers and pupils. The MEP and others claimed that the power of the microcomputer could be used to help children acquire facility in manipulating and interpreting information. There was limited evidence to support this contention, although there was an increasing awareness among teachers of what might be possible given suitable resources and experience in various subject studies and school libraries. If pupils could call up information services and gather knowledge and information for themselves, this could, it was suggested, change pupils' and teachers' outlooks on these resources. The paucity and high cost of telephone links and the lack of access to suitable databases together with inexperience on the part of teachers, were all obstacles to development. It should also be remembered that the proper use of IT in this context represented a radical change in traditional practices of information handling in schools. Where good examples of organisation and interpreting information were observed, they provided pupils with insights which transcended a particular area or subject of study.

Problem solving skills

Many MEP products could encourage problem solving skills in areas of the curriculum such as mathematics, science, computer studies, electronics and technology. Except in some mathematics classrooms, few secondary subject classes aimed at developing these abilities with the help of MEP's CBL materials. In computer studies, however, the increase in the number of machines available resulted in more programming and some excellent problem solving tasks being undertaken by pupils. These skills were also fostered by courses, such as MFA, where pupils were encouraged to use a 'system approach' to solving technological control problems. This involved consideration being given to the function of a complete unit, rather than the detailed examination of its components and construction. This approach seemed to increase the level of interest in girls who appeared to find a 'component approach' uninteresting.

Creativity and imagination

Creativity and imagination were encouraged through the use of MEP LOGO materials and a number of other MEP products. For example, in one special school pupils worked in groups on a demanding task in which they created an animated cartoon set to music. This generated great interest and stimulated enthusiasm and sustained effort. In other schools, computer materials encouraged speculative skills in mathematics.

Although there were examples of creative uses of the new technology in art, design and music, these were rare and generally at an embryonic stage. Some teachers felt that new technology equipment in these fields allowed pupils to compose and experiment with ideas, uninhibited by their own lack of drawing, painting or musical performance skills. EDFAX and similar programs that allowed pupils to generate teletext-type graphics motivated some pupils who had seldom shown interest in art. Using music packages, groups of pupils worked for long periods of time composing pieces and devising sequential patterns.

Personal and social skills
For some pupils personal and social skills developed and self-esteem was improved as a result of success in using the new technology. Where pupils were using IT they were often more readily able to discuss issues with adults. In many cases teachers saw their classroom role changing and appeared to be moving with their pupils towards a situation where expertise and problem solving were shared. Group work was more evident in such situations, although examples of pupils becoming isolated with computers were mentioned by teachers. Boys often tended to dominate girls when groups were using computers unless the teacher took care to guard against this. A number of schools had instituted 'girls only' days for their computer clubs as a strategy to overcome the problem. These and other 'equal opportunities' strategies were encouraged by the EOC project based in one LEA.

In nearly every case pupils handled expensive equipment with care and respect. There was only one case of deliberate misuse noted during the survey, although there were several examples of theft.

Skills – primary schools

Communication skills
Many of the points raised in the above section on secondary schools also applied to the primary sector. Teachers suggested that the whole range of communication skills – talking, listening, reading and writing – was extended through using computers and there was some evidence to support these claims. Discussion was an essential part of many programs where decision making was required, for example in simulations, or when using LOGO. Although the level of discussion varied, it was often the case that normally quiet or reticent children contributed on equal terms with their more vocal peers. There were other examples of improved perform-ance in writing and in reading, when sustained effort produced work of improved quantity and quality. Children using MICROWRITERs to check and correct their own and each other's work and pupils' hand written work was also said to have improved. Unfortunately not all schools with computers possessed printers. This limited the value of wordprocessing programs since pupils were unable to obtain a paper copy of what they had produced. To counter this some RICs encouraged some schools by loaning them printers. In one school two 9-year old boys were using EDWORD to revise a piece of writing which they had done jointly

the previous day. The passage, which was about 600 words long, was intended for inclusion in a class newspaper. The quality of the discussion; the critical consideration of word choice; and the facility with which they used the word processor to try different arrangements were all high.

Problem solving skills
Although in the best practice primary school children have long been involved with problem solving as a learning strategy, the use of computers and the related technology offered opportunities for more specific problem solving skills to be used. Prediction, deciding on a strategy, and reflecting on and discussing results, were some of the skills noted. Projects which encouraged a logical approach to solving problems had the support of MEP. This support came not only through the in-service packs but also through the production of related materials and software including simulations, LOGO and, the use of a computer to control models. In one school a group of infants were using a floor turtle so that each had a different job. They worked as a team and then changed jobs. Their tasks introduced them to the mathematical concepts of estimation and measurement. In another school, a class of fourth year pupils demonstrated programs they had produced in LOGO to illustrate their own written stories about a chase across a roof. They used concepts of distance and time in order to program sprites (small symbols made to move around the computer screen).

Creativity
Certain MEP packages promoted a range of creative abilities when well implemented by the teacher. They encouraged pupils to be creative and imaginative in their use of language in written work, and also in mathematics. Many schools had yet to move away from practising basic skills, but the NPP tried to encourage a more open approach.

Personal and social skills
Many children seemed to acquire more confidence through using the computer. Teachers frequently quoted examples of those who had lacked confidence socially or who had previously found it difficult to write, read and take part in activities on equal terms with their peers, becoming more confident as a result of using IT in their learning. In one school a boy became the recognised expert on the making and control of a vehicle and, at the same time, had become interested in recording his work using a word-processor. Although of below average attainment, his written work had increased from two or three badly written lines, to a sustained piece of writing which, when printed, compared favourably with that of more able class-mates.

Although the MEP cannot claim sole responsibility for such positive aspects, a contribution has nevertheless been made through the enthusiastic approach of those involved and the high quality of some of the materials produced.

Knowledge and understanding – secondary schools
There was evidence that the use of some computer programs, many of

them not necessarily funded by MEP, helped pupils to gain knowledge and understand ideas more easily. Pupils' learning was enhanced because they were able to manipulate data and text at first hand; teach themselves from handbooks; or present their solutions or problems in novel ways. There were good, but rare, examples seen in several subjects in the curriculum. In some home economics for example, pupils were able to apply newly gained knowledge about diet to planning specific meals, and in physics simulation programs made concepts such as wave motion more comprehensible. In control technology, a systems approach enabled pupils to visualise situations more clearly and to apply technological concepts to solving real problems. In mathematics, programs were observed which had been designed to enable pupils to understand ideas and concepts which would normally be very difficult, for most pupils without a computer. However, lessons were also seen where pupils might have gained a better understanding of concepts without the use of a computer.

Knowledge and understanding – primary schools

By combining the use of the computer with first hand experiences and other sources as recommended by NPP, many schools had added a new dimension to their work through recording data, retrieving information and presenting results. Likewise the use of LOGO and the developments in control technology motivated children to tackle problems in new ways and often to set themselves the next task when one was finished. Teachers receptive to the INSET and curriculum initiatives emanating from the NPP used the computer to find ways of presenting work so that pupils acquired knowledge and understanding. A commercial program which simulated the finding and raising of a Tudor warship, the *Mary Rose*, was selected by the MEP Primary Project term as an example of a simulation program that could be used to enhance topic work. This was observed being used in an INSET course and later followed up in schools. The results were encouraging. In one class children had plotted their finds on three dimensional grids; had gained a sound knowledge of the problems of working under the sea; and had researched the period in great detail. Their written work was lively and often established for the reader the excitement of diving or finding treasure, reflecting the computer simulation. Art work and model making added to the displays and illustrated the depth of study undertaken. In another school, in another region, work in mathematics, based on the same program, had included compass bearings, shape, co-ordinates and angles, these topics being reinforced by the computer work. Some children (having carefully researched the background) had recorded interviews pretending to be members of the crew. Although they were unable to visit the real *Mary Rose*, a visit was to be made to a ship built in the 1860s at Hartlepool; the teacher felt they knew so much about the Tudor ship that they would be able to make comparisons. In both schools the teachers and pupils were enthusiastic and deeply involved in the work.

A great deal of further work remains to be done especially in respect of the need to provide a full range of suitable software which is both challenging in its nature and capable of being integrated into teaching and learning patterns across the full curriculum spectrum. Furthermore, as with everything new in education, the in-service implications for the teaching profession – notably across subject boundaries – have yet to be implemented adequately.

Nevertheless, it is fair to say that the advent of microelectronics in schools has provided the occasion for an historic shift of emphasis in teaching and learning patterns: the age of the computer must find a reflection in curriculum structure and in curriculum core content.

CHAPTER 16

TECHNOLOGY AND THE CURRICULUM

Free secondary education for all as envisaged in the 1944 Education Act had left unquestioned the 'tripartite' assumption that children at secondary level could, at least theoretically, be selected into three groups – a grammar school group, a technical school group and the new 'secondary modern' group.

In practice however the technical school concept did not develop fully and in the immediate post-war period progress on a true tripartite system remained bogged down by financial stringencies, shortages of materials, difficulties over teacher supply and the overriding necessity to raise the school leaving age.

Following comprehensivisation, courses in technical subjects found a place in the new system, but the role of technology itself received scant thought in curriculum terms and 'common core' premisses.

This glaring gap in general provision was alleviated by the further education and technical college system, but this operated principally at post secondary school level.

Although courses under the heading of Craft, Design and Technology gradually found a place at secondary level, it was not until 1982 that the government initiated definitive measures in the form of the Technical and Vocational Education Initiative.

Again this plan suffered from being grafted onto the secondary school system, often with undertones of suspicion and resentment. Undefined cap-touching references to technology had begun to appear in curriculum documents from the mid-1970s, but a fully developed school curriculum plan incorporating the essences of technology remained a long way off.

City Technology Colleges

Late in 1986 however, the Gordian knots of local control, professional attitudes and industrial apathy were suddenly severed by a radical new proposal from the Secretary of State. The core of this proposal was the intention to establish a centrally funded network of 20 city technology schools or colleges, which would provide a secondary education with strong technological elements.

The characteristics of the new colleges were described as follows:

1. They will normally cater for 11–18 year olds.

2. They will be registered independent schools, subject to inspection by Her Majesty's Inspectorate.

3. They will charge no fees.

4. The promoters will own (or lease) and run them, and receive grants on conditions agreed with the Secretary of State.

5. The promoters will make a substantial contribution towards the costs.

6. They will offer a broad curriculum, with the strong technical and practical element which is essential preparation for the changing demands of adult and working life in an advanced industrial society.

7. They will seek to develop the qualities of enterprise, self-reliance and responsibility which young people need for adult life and work and for citizenship.

8. They will be set up in urban areas, including the disadvantaged inner cities.

9. They will aim to secure the highest possible standards of achievement, both academically and in other ways.

A New Choice of School

In *A New Choice of School* (DES 1986), the curriculum implications of the proposed city technology colleges were spelled out. Assuming an institution with 1,000 places and a teacher/pupil ratio of 15.4:1, a possible timetable for the first three years (11–14 age range) might consist of seven sections:

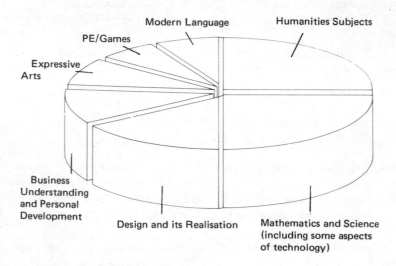

Time allocations for 11–14
Over the 11–14 three-year period the time allocations could be:

	Percentage
Mathematics and Science	25
Design and its realisation	20
Humanities subjects	25
Other courses	30

(Differentiation within the framework would be allowed for according to the needs of individual pupils).

Time allocations for 14–16
For the 14–16 two-year period the 'common core' elements would be retained and the addition of limited choice options would result in a 'curriculum cake' of nine slices:

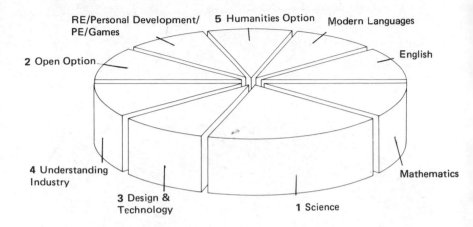

Points to be noted from the curriculum proposals for the 14–16 age group are:

1. Science occupies 20 per cent of the week; it might be taught as separate subject, in an integrated way or as double science.

2. The open option will include a wide range of subjects, which will vary with schools' particular strengths: e.g., history, geography, RE, a second foreign language, music, home economics, computer studies and economics.

3. The design and technology course will include elements of CDT, technology, art, computing and information technology.

4. This course will be organised on a basic of units or modules including industrial design as well as the financial and economic aspects of industry and commerce.

5. This option will include subjects such as economics, geography and history.

Except for the double science allocation it was proposed that all subjects/courses should receive an allocation of approximately 10 per cent of the week.)

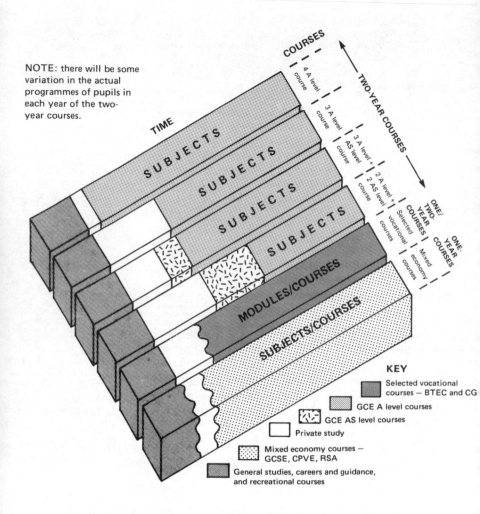

NOTE: there will be some variation in the actual programmes of pupils in each year of the two-year courses.

KEY

- Selected vocational courses – BTEC and CG
- GCE A level courses
- GCE AS level courses
- Private study
- Mixed economy courses – GCSE, CPVE, RSA
- General studies, careers and guidance, and recreational courses

PROPOSALS FOR THE SIXTH FORM

In the sixth form it was proposed that combinations of one-year, one or two-years and two-year courses should be provided. These would cover Royal Society of Arts examinations, the Certificate of Pre-Vocational Education and the new General Certificate of Secondary Education examination at Ordinary, Advanced and Advanced Supplementary level.

Additionally, one or two-year vocational courses could be undertaken leading to Business and Technician Education Council, or City and Guilds of London Institute examinations.

Presented diagramatically, the timetable construction blocks appeared as shown on p 114.

The proposed establishment of city technology colleges raises many fundamental questions about the central influence and control of education and the role of the LEAs quite apart from the curricular suggestions here outlined.

These topics lie beyond the scope of this study: with a clutch of CTCs in the pipeline, it is a question of 'wait and see'.

CHAPTER 17

THE NATIONAL CURRICULUM AND THE 1987 EDUCATION BILL

The reorganisation of the educational system initiated in 1965 by the introduction of comprehensive schooling had inevitably led, as has been demonstrated in previous sections, to a sustained effort to unlock the secret garden of the curriculum.

Yet a dozen years after the famous comprehensive circular of 1965, it had still been possible to remark that: 'we have no educational system, we only have schools'.

This lack of structure was similarly criticised by Kenneth Baker in 1987, when he labelled the educational scene as 'maverick'. Certainly the only visible factor at secondary level which gives an indication of a national curriculum is the delineation provided by the syllabus requirements of the external examination boards. Indeed, the syllabuses and schemes of work of very many secondary schools are encapsulated within the framework of future examination requirements.

In practical terms the ground for manoeuvre has been wide: the principal problem for schools has been the fact that the existing examination system has been obliged to serve two functions. It is both a final assessment examination for the majority of pupils and also a qualifying examination for those pupils who wish to proceed to some form of higher education.

Hence arose the understandable aim of Sir Keith Joseph in 1984 to wrench the system from its prognostic connotations for the few to an achievement record for the many.

The ensuing declarations in *Better Schools* in 1985 and in the

Education Act of 1986 can nevertheless, in retrospect, be seen as largely 'nuts and bolts' exercises which related to the scaffolding of education. The superstructure was to arrive suddenly in 1987 when the Secretary of State heralded an increasingly interventionist stance in his speech of 9 January 1987.

Kenneth Baker's 1987 speech

The venue was again the North of England Education Conference and on this occasion Kenneth Baker pointed to the urgent need to improve quality and standards in primary and secondary schools. In his speech he declared:

> Although its overall purpose and its range are widely agreed for the compulsory period, there is as yet considerable doubt about how broad the primary curriculum could and should be, and no agreement about what and how much choice there should be for the last two compulsory secondary years.
>
> Nor is there yet broad agreement about the balance between the elements of the curriculum, or about the objectives of each element, despite good progress towards agreement in mathematics, science and foreign languages.

The way forward, he declared, lay in:

> Establishing a national curriculum which works through national criteria for each subject area of the curriculum.

This declared developmental policy for education at a national level was reiterated and reinforced in the Conservative Party election manifesto of May 1987, when it was made clear that a specific national core curriculum was envisaged. The national curriculum would be detailed and would be executed through three elements:

1. There would be published and prescribed syllabuses for the national core curriculum. This curriculum would include, among other subjects, defined objectives for the teaching of mathematics, English and science.

2. 'Attainment levels' for individual areas of experience would be set for the ages of 7, 11, 14, and 16.

3. Forms of 'assessment' would be outlined for the evaluation of attainment levels and the recording of pupils' progress.

The National Curriculum 5–16

The return of a Conservative government with a large majority, following the general election in June 1987, was taken as an indication of public endorsement of the manifesto proposals and the Department of Education and Science immediately issued a consultation document under the heading of *The National Curriculum 5–16*. This document was broadly in line with the manifesto proposals and comment was invited on its contents, within a three-month period, prior to proposed legislation in the form of a new major Education Act.

The consultation document asserted that:

1. Pupils are entitled to the same opportunities, wherever they attend school.

2. Standards of attainment must be raised throughout England and Wales.

These new 'Standards of Attainment' would be achieved, in the view of the document, by:

(a) A common core curriculum which would ensure that all pupils studied a balanced and broad range of subjects throughout their compulsory school period.
(b) The setting up of assessment arrangements which would give *'clear objectives for what children over the full range of ability should be able to achieve'*.
(c) The provision of a guarantee that pupils would all have access to the same curriculum containing the key elements which all pupils need to learn.
(d) A check on progress at set stages throughout a pupil's career.

It was further maintained that the proposed national curriculum would ensure that pupils could move from one area of the country to another, without a considerable disruption in the content of their education: here the consultation document clearly echoed the 1977 HMI *Curriculum 11–16* papers, which had commented upon the educational disadvantages of parental mobility in a decentralised education system.

Finally, the consultation document maintained that a national and publicly defined curriculum would render schools more readily 'accountable' to society, and also enable teachers to evaluate their own work more systematically.

The content of the National Curriculum

As indicated in the Conservative election manifesto the consultation document proposed a basic core curriculum composed of English, mathematics and science, 'to be followed by all pupils during compulsory schooling'. The majority of time at the primary school level should be given to these three core subjects. At the secondary school level, study of the three core subjects should continue and should occupy approximately 30–40 per cent of school time.

In addition to the core subjects, the consultation document proposed that there should be a set of *foundation subjects* consisting of technology, history, a modern foreign language (not at primary level), geography, art, physical education and music. Taken together it was estimated that the total prescribed curriculum would occupy between 80–90 per cent of the school timetable. The consultation document commented that the place of religious education in schools was already secured by statute and that it must form an essential part of the curriculum.

Complementing such 'additional subjects' as second foreign language study and home economics, it was suggested that a further number of subjects could be assimilated at 'theme' level (i.e. health education, information technology), without infringing upon the foundation subjects time allocation.

Curriculum working groups

The extremely tight consultation timetable was maintained by the issue, one month after the consultation document, of 'letters of guidance' for the newly established curriculum working groups for two of the core subjects, namely mathematics and science. Letters of guidance asked for the core working groups to provide an interim report before the end of the calendar year. The letters explicitly stated that a detailed programme of study should be outlined describing:

> the content, skills and processes which all pupils need to be taught so that they can develop the knowledge and understanding they will need to progress through school and eventually to adult life and employment. [DES News, 24 August 1987]

The letters further commented that the Secretary of State was asking for a statement of attainment targets:

which pupils of different abilities should be able to achieve by the end of the school year in which they reach the key ages.

These attainment targets were to allow scope for the very able, those of average ability, and the less able to show what they could do. However, so far as possible, the working groups were asked *'to avoid having different attainment levels for children of different levels of ability'*. Instead it was suggested that there should be set targets for each of the key ages, which could be assessed at a range of levels.

The consultation document concluded by remarking that its proposals:

> 'represent a major step forward towards the common aims for compulsory education which have emerged from the debate about the curriculum begun ten years ago and recorded in *Better Schools*. The challenge for the education service is to raise standards through the full and successful implementation of the national curriculum – to the point where every pupil is studying for, and being regularly assessed against, worthwhile attainment targets in all the essential foundation subjects, and where all members of the community with an interest in the country's education services are able to inform themselves properly about its objectives and achievements.'

The promised Education Reform Bill was published on November 20, 1987: as a result of strenuous lobbying over the consultation document, the proposed time allocations for the National Curriculum were left unspecified. In other respects the Bill followed faithfully the National Curriculum consultation document.

The year 1987 thus marked the final unlocking of the secret garden, its formalisation and the bounding of its territories.

Implications of the Education Reform Bill for teachers

The national core curriculum plans will face teachers with a range of problems and challenges. The decline of age-related and subject based testing at primary level which followed the disappearance of the eleven-plus examination left teachers free to continue with the overriding aim of developing to the full the many-faceted potentialities of each pupil. This constituted a great step forward, since in the eleven-plus era, even the best teachers were constrained to focus attention upon testable items, often to the extent of practice in verbal reasoning and 'intelligence' questions.

The prospect therefore of the imposition of national testing at the ages of 7, 11, 14 and 16 must give rise to a serious anxiety about the possible stultification of the curriculum process and its lapse into a process of diseducation. Thus the phrase 'payment by results' has now achieved a new respectability and occasionally appears but one step removed from that ministerial dictum which has echoed down the century: 'if the new system is not cheap it shall be efficient; if it is not efficient it shall be cheap.'

These ghosts of payment by results are revived today by the notions of 'benchmarks', 'useful knowledge' and 'educational clutter'. All enterprises are surrounded by constraints: if a national curriculum with national standards is to be proposed as a declared educational aim, then the overall restraint of available resources must be faced. The famous legend of the DES 'nothing is to be construed as implying government commitment to the provision of additional resources' cannot be left to stand since national standards demand national and equable resources. Apart from deficiencies in the provision of physical resources and learning materials there remains a serious and continuing shortage in the supply of able and well qualified teachers of mathematics and science, which constitute two of the proposed 'key' areas of the primary and secondary curriculum.

But the dangers of a nationally tested curriculum if thus recognised can nevertheless be turned to positive action by planned approaches from the teaching profession:

1. The introduction of tested elements must not lead to the trivialisation of individual study areas. It is urgently necessary to prepare for the inclusion of testable items as an element in overall planned schemes of work: thus the tests should not appear in the form of discontinuous external 'papers'. It must also be stressed that the testable elements must not be divorced from curriculum obligations in the spheres of attitudes, values and personal and social development.

2. Tested elements should be considered as running across curriculum areas and to varying extents they should reflect a whole staff policy. There is therefore a need for a 'whole school' curriculum document.

3. Tested elements should not be perceived in a pass/fail sense. The purpose of the tested elements must be made explicit to children, teachers, parents and outside bodies. Diagnoses of learning difficulties, descriptions of attainments and performance can constitute an acceptable face of testing: benchmarks for possible failure for pupils (and teachers) cannot.

4. Individual subject schemes of work will need careful and consistent planning at LEA level, at whole school level, at departmental level, and at individual teacher level. Thus it will be necessary to consider 'testing' implications not only in relation to the broad curriculum prospectus presented to parents and governors, but also as part of the more detailed teaching steps which specify limited but progressive objectives.

5. With specific objectives in view the teacher needs to analyse what might be the most appropriate subject content (involving testable elements) and then plan the appropriate learning/ teaching sequences. Most importantly provision needs to be made for an *evaluation* of the programme at regular intervals. *Feedback* as far as the tested benchmarks are concerned, will be automatically provided by the benchmark results, but it will be very necessary to consider how the results contribute to a meaningful profile of the performance and achievements and the talents and the competences of the individual pupil. Needless to say, the *interpretation* of the benchmark scores will need the most careful consideration.

The crucial problem remains – *how is the curriculum to be delivered?* Plans for a common core, for a national curriculum, for benchmarks, agreed objectives and standards all count for nothing unless the classroom and the teacher/pupil relationships are sound in principle and in everyday practice. Curriculum documents and curriculum discussion over the last ten years have referred obliquely to classroom situations and the LEA expenditure surveys by HMI have highlighted the physical conditions and the resources with which teachers must work.

It would be out of place here to attempt a detailed analysis of classroom method but all evidence points to the same basic points which make for success or failure:

1. Effective leadership is vital both at headteacher and at departmental level.

2. In spite of national curriculum and common core considerations, what is taught and the way in which it is taught and learnt, must match the individual and collective needs of pupils as perceived at grassroots level.

3. The pupils must always be involved actively in their learning situations.

4. Teachers need to have accurate perceptions and expectations of their pupils and their capabilities.

5. Hard work, differentiation of tasks, variations of pace and the teacher's own enthusiasms all contribute towards effective and meaningful learning.

Above all, for a school to flourish and achieve its curricular and its pastoral objectives, it must display a sense of shared principles and values.

As with political ventures, the educational enterprise itself sails on largely uncharted waters; the landmarks we spy and the harbours we approach are those which we choose to set for ourselves. Educational judgements are never value free.

PUBLICATIONS FOR FURTHER STUDY

DES and priced HMI publications are obtainable from HMSO Publications Centre (PO Box 276, London SW8 5DT), from HMSO Bookshop Agents, or from bookshops.

The following titles contain useful material, both on overall curriculum matters and on individual subject topics:

1. *Curriculum from 5–16*, 1985. Curriculum Matters No 2.
2. *Curriculum 11–16. A review of progress*. A joint study by HMI and five LEAs 1981.
3. *Curriculum 11–16. Towards a Statement of Entitlement*. Curricular reappraisal in action, 1983.
4. *English from 5–16*, 1984. Curriculum Matters No 1.
5. *General Certificate of Secondary Education: the National Criteria*. Subject specific criteria statements, 1985.
6. *Gifted Children in Middle and Comprehensive Secondary Schools*, 1977.
7. *Girls and Science*, 1980. HMI Matters for Discussion No 13.
8. *Health Education 5–16*, 1986.
9. *History in the Primary and Secondary Years*. An HMI view, 1985.
10. *Home Economics from 5–16*, 1985. Curriculum Matters No 5.
11. *Mathematics from 5–16*, 1985. Curriculum Matters No 3.
12. *Microcomputers and Mathematics in Schools*, 1985
13. *Mixed Ability Work in Comprehensive Schools*. HMI Matters for Discussion No 6, 1978.
14. *Music from 5–16*, 1985. Curriculum Matters No 4.
15. *Records of Achievement at 16*. Some examples of current practice, 1985.
16. *The School Curriculum*, 1981.
17. *Science 5–16, A Statement of Policy*, 1985.
18. *Technology and School Science*. An HMI enquiry, 1985.
19. *Ten Good Schools*, 1977. HMI Matters for Discussion No 1.
20. *A View of the Curriculum*, 1980. HMI Matters for Discussion No 11.

SUMMARY OF THE 1986 EDUCATION ACT

Part 1 Introductory

Section 1 provides a fresh statutory framework for making and amending the instruments and articles of government for all schools by the LEA.

Section 2 sets out the procedures an LEA will have to follow when making new instruments and articles of government or when the governing body makes proposals to alter them.

Part II School government

Sections 3–15 make new provision for the composition of school governing bodies with four basic categories of governors: parents, local education authority representatives, teachers (and the head teacher) and others co-opted by the rest of the governors, at least one of whom is required to be from the local business community. The provisions will be incorporated in instruments of government.

Section 3 specifies the basic composition of governing bodies for county, controlled and maintained special schools of various sizes as follows:

Pupil numbers	Parents	LEA	Headteacher	Teacher	Co-opted (or, for controlled schools: foundation/ co-opted)	Total
up to 99	2	2	1	1	3 (2/1)	9
100–299	3	3	1	1	4 (3/1)	12
300–599	4	4	1	2	5 (4/1)	16
600 or more	5	5	1	2	6 (4/2)	19

Section 4 re-enacts the relevant provisions of Section 2 of the 1980 Act and sets out the numbers and categories of governors for aided and special agreement schools. Foundation governors, with at least one being a parent of a pupil at the school, will be in the majority. Other governors will be parents, teachers, the head teacher and LEA representatives.

Section 5 deals with the case of schools where insufficient parents stand for election as parent governors or where the LEA decide that elections are not practicable for either a hospital school or a school where at least half the pupils are boarders. In such a case the other governors will appoint the necessary parent governors from among persons who have a child at the school or, failing that, children of compulsory age. They may not appoint an elected member, an employee or a co-opted member of any education committee of the authority.

Section 6 provides for the representation of the local business community on governing bodies.

Section 7 enables a minor authority to appoint a governor to a county or controlled primary school serving its area; the district health authority a governor to a maintained special school in a hospital; and an appropriate voluntary organisation, one or two governors to a maintained special school.

Section 8 provides for governors to have a four-year term of office. Governors may resign their office or, in the case of appointed (not elected or co-opted) governors, may be removed from office early only by those who appoint them. The Secretary of State will have power to supplement the Section's provisions concerning the proceedings of governing bodies in regulations.

Section 9 (and Schedule 1) specify the arrangements for the grouping of schools under a single governing body.

Section 10 requires the LEA to obtain the Secretary of State's consent to grouping of schools unless the group is to consist of only two primary schools, provided both schools serve substantially the same area, neither is a special school and, in Wales, there is no significant difference between them in the use of the Welsh language.

Section 11 sets out the arrangements for the constitution of the governing body to be viewed from time to time in the light of changing pupil numbers.

Section 12 (and Schedule 2) require an LEA to set up an appropriately constituted temporary governing body to deal with the many decisions needed before a new school opens.

Section 13 sets out the action that the LEA will have to take, or may take on a contingency basis, to vary instruments of government to reflect changes in circumstances of a school.

Section 14 sets out the procedure for a governing body to reduce its numbers if, following a change of circumstances, it has more members of a particular category than provided for in the instrument of government.

Section 15 deals with various miscellaneous matters, in particular the election of parent and teacher governors. The LEA will be required to take all reasonable steps to see that all parents of registered pupils are informed of governor vacancies and told that they are entitled to stand as candidates and vote. Elections will be by secret ballot and must, in the case of parent governors, include the opportunity for voting by post. No one under the age of 18 will be eligible for election, appointment or co-option as a governor.

Part III Organisation and functions

Sections 16–42 relate to the allocation of functions between the governing body, the LEA and the head teacher, to be specified in articles of government.

Section 16 provides for the governing body to control the conduct of the school subject to other statutory provisions and for the Secretary of State to make regulations prescribing circumstances where a requirement for the governing body to be consulted may be varied in cases of urgency.

Section 17 makes it a duty of the LEA to make and keep up to date a written statement of its policy in relation to the secular curriculum, copies of which will be available for inspection in schools.

Section 18 makes it a duty of the governing body of a county, controlled or maintained special school to consider the LEA's policy (with regard to matters other than sex education) for the secular curriculum; what should be the general aims of the secular curriculum for the school; and how, if at all, in their opinion, the LEA's statement should be modified for their school. The governing body will have to consult the head teacher and also the LEA when considering these matters. They will also have to give a copy of their statement to the LEA and head teacher, and it will be available for inspection at the school. The governing body will be required to review their aims for the curriculum if a school's circumstances change. The governing body will have to consider separately, while having regard to the LEA's statement under Section 17 of this Act, whether sex education should form part of the curriculum of the school. They will have a duty to maintain a written statement of how sex education should be taught, and to set down any decision they may make for it not to form part of the curriculum. Again, the statement will be available for inspection at the school.

The head teacher will be responsible for determining and organising the curriculum within the school in a way that is compatible with the policy of the LEA or, if incompatible with that policy, with that policy as modified by the governing body. So far as sex education is concerned, the head teacher will have to ensure that the curriculum is compatible with the governing body's policy, provided that this does not conflict with the syllabus of any public examination.

Any persons connected with the community served by the school or the relevant chief officer of police may make representations to the governing body and head teacher about the curriculum which they will be required to consider.

Section 19 provides for the governing body of an aided or special agreement school to have control of the curriculum, having regard to the LEA's policy. The head teacher will be allocated such functions that will, subject to the resources available, enable him or her to determine and organise the curriculum. He or she will be responsible for seeing it is followed within the school.

Section 20 requires the Secretary of State to make regulations regarding the availability of information to parents about the syllabuses followed by their children in schools. Governing bodies will have the responsibility for ensuring that such information is available in the form and manner specified and at the times prescribed.

Section 21 makes it a duty of the LEA to determine school times and the dates of school terms and holidays for county, controlled and maintained special schools and a duty of the governing body to do so for aided and special agreement schools.

Section 22 makes it a duty of each head teacher to determine measures to be taken with a view to:

– promoting, among pupils, self-discipline and proper regard for authority;
– encouraging good behaviour on the part of pupils;
– securing that the standards of behaviour of pupils is acceptable;
– regulating the conduct of pupils;

in accordance with any written statement of general principles provided for him by the governing body.

Sections 23–25 set out procedures to deal with exclusions. Where a pupil is excluded from school for more than five days (in aggregate) in any one term, or if his or her exclusion would result in the loss of an opportunity to take any public examination, the head teacher will have to inform the LEA and the governing body without delay and to comply with any direction given by either for the immediate reinstatement of the pupil. The governing body and the LEA will have to inform each other of any direction given to the head teacher.

When a pupil is excluded from school permanently or indefinitely and the governing body do not intend to direct the head teacher to reinstate him or her, the LEA will have a duty to decide what should happen; inform the governing body and the head teacher of their decision; and when they decide in favour of reinstatement to give such direction as they consider appropriate.

In the case of aided and special agreement schools, only the governing body will have the right permanently to exclude a pupil and they will have to notify the LEA at once.

Section 26 (and Schedule 3) provide for a right of appeal for the parents of a pupil who has been permanently excluded from school, and for the governing body if the LEA orders his reinstatement. Such appeals will be made to appeal committees constituted under Part 1 of Schedule 2 to the 1980 Act and the decision reached will be binding on the persons concerned.

In the case of a pupil expelled from an aided or special agreement school, the LEA will not be directly involved and the appeals process can start as soon as the governing body has endorsed the head teacher's decision.

Section 27 accommodates local appeal agreements in cases not covered by Section 26.

Section 28 gives the LEA power to take such steps as they consider necessary to prevent the breakdown of discipline at a county, controlled or maintained special school as a result of action either by pupils or their parents.

Section 29 requires the LEA to give each governing body an annual statement of the running costs of their school and to make available to them funds which the governing body can spend at their discretion on books, equipment, stationery and such other headings of expenditure as may be specified by the LEA or prescribed by the Secretary of State. The governing body will be able to delegate to the head teacher their powers for spending specific sums.

Sections 30–31 require the governing body to prepare an annual report to parents and to hold an annual parents' meeting at which this report and other aspects of the school's life may be discussed. Parents may pass formal resolutions on matters for the attention of the LEA, governing body or head teacher.

Section 32 enables the LEA to require reports from the governing body or the head teacher; and the governing body to require reports from the head teacher.

Section 33 sets out new requirements for consultation over the arrangement for admissions to schools. Where the LEA is responsible for deciding school admissions they will have to consult the governors annually as to whether the arrangments are satisfactory, and before any alteration. Where the governors are responsible for admission procedures they will have to consult the governing body.

Sections 34–41 set out a new statutory framework for the appointment and dismissal of staff in county, controlled, special agreement and maintained special schools.

Section 34 requires the LEA, within specified constraints, to set the complement of teaching and non-teaching staff at each school. This determines the appointments procedure to be followed in individual cases.

Section 35 makes the LEA's general control of appointment and dismissal of staff subject to the provisions in Sections 36–41 for involving the governing body.

Section 36 requires the constitution of a selection panel in relation to the appointment of a head teacher (or deputy head teacher if this procedure is used). The LEA and governing body are to have at least three members each on the selection panel; and articles of government may provide for the governing body to have a majority. The Secretary of State will be able to make provision in regulations as to the meetings and proceedings of the selection panel.

Section 37 prohibits the LEA from appointing anyone as head teacher unless recommended by the selection panel. The LEA will have to advertise the vacancy widely and the selection panel will then be responsible for the selection process.

If the recommended applicant is not acceptable to the LEA or if the panel cannot agree on a recommendation, the panel will repeat all or some of the steps in the selection process, including requesting the LEA to readvertise; and if the selection panel does not produce a recommendation within a reasonable period the LEA will be able in any case to readvertise.

The Chief Education Officer will have the right to attend all parts of the selection process and give advice.

If a head teacher post is actually vacant, the LEA will be required to appoint an acting head teacher, after consulting the governing body, until a full appointment made through the selection process takes effect.

Section 38 sets out the proposed arrangements for appointing other staff. The LEA will decide whether a vacancy shall remain on the complement.

If it is to be filled, the LEA will have to advertise the post unless they decide on redeployment. For an advertised post, the governing body or its representatives will be responsible for selecting and interviewing candidates and making a recommendation to the LEA.

If the LEA accepts the recommendation, an appointment will be made; if the LEA rejects the recommendation or the governing body cannot agree on a recommendation to the LEA, the process will repeat itself.

If, however, the LEA decides to fill the vacancy by redeployment, the governing body will be able to give the LEA a specification after consultation with the head teacher. The LEA will have to consult the governing body when considering an appointment for the post. If under this procedure the LEA makes an appointment with which the governing body disagrees, the matter will have to be reported to the next meeting of the appropriate education committee.

Section 39 specifies that the procedure for the appointment of a deputy head will be either that for the appointment of a head teacher or that for the appointment of other staff (described in Sections 37 and 38 respectively). In addition, where the head teacher of a school using the first procedure was not on the appointment panel, he or she will be entitled to be present at all meetings, including the interview, to give advice, and will have to be consulted before an appointment is made.

Section 40 provides for the clerk of the governing body of a county or maintained special school to be appointed or dismissed by the LEA in consultation with the governing body. The appointment and dismissal of the clerk to the governing body of a controlled or special agreement school will be determined by the articles of government for each school.

Section 41 requires the LEA to consult the governing body and the head teacher before dismissing a member of staff; allowing them premature retirement; or redeploying them. The LEA will also have to consult the governing body and head teacher before extending a person's probationary period or deciding whether it has been successfully completed. The governing body and head teacher will each have the power to suspend a member of staff. They will have to inform the LEA and each other immediately and end the suspension if directed to do so by the LEA.

Section 42 provides for the governing body to control the use of school premises outside school sessions subject to any direction given by the LEA. In doing so they will have to have regard to the desirability of the premises being made available by members of the community served by the school.

Part IV Miscellaneous

Section 43 lays a general duty on all those concerned in the government of an institution of further or higher education to secure, so far as is reasonably practicable, freedom of speech within the law for members, students and employees of the establishment and for visiting speakers. A central part of the duty turns on a code of practice, to be drawn up in each institution, covering the procedures applying to the agreement of meetings and other activities, and the conduct required in relation to them.

Section 44 requires LEAs, governing bodies and head teachers to forbid the pursuit of partisan political activities among primary aged pupils at school and the promotion of partisan political views among all pupils.

Section 45 requires LEAs, governing bodies and head teachers to take such steps as are reasonably practicable to secure that where political issues legitimately arise in the course of school lessons or during extra-curricular activities organised by the school off the premises, pupils are offered a balanced presentation of opposing views.

Section 46 requires LEAs, governing bodies and head teachers to take such steps as are reasonably practicable to secure that any sex education which is offered encourages pupils to have due regard to moral considerations and the value of family life.

Section 47 provides for the abolition of corporal punishment. It affects pupils attending maintained schools, non-maintained special schools, and voluntary aided schools. It also covers pupils receiving education otherwise than at school and those who hold a place in an independent school under the Assisted Places Scheme.

Section 48 makes similar provisions for Scotland and amending the Education (Scotland) Act 1980.

Section 49 enables the Secretary of State to make regulations, after consulting local authority and teacher associations, for the appraisal of school and college teachers' performance in their duties and related activities.

Section 50 empowers the Secretary of State to provide by regulations for the payment of grant to LEAs and others for teacher training. Grant will be payable only for training approved by the Secretary of State.

Section 51 supersedes Section 31 of the Education Act 1980. It will provide a new framework for the recoupment of costs between LEAs. The Secretary of State will be empowered to give directions, both particular and general, as to the rates of recoupment. In the case of prescribed non-advanced further education or primary education in hospitals for under five year olds there will no longer be the need to seek the consent of the authority to which the pupil or student belongs for recoupment purposes.

Section 52 re-enacts relevant provisions of the 1980 Act relating to recoupment between LEAs and education authorities in Scotland.

Section 53 amends Section 51 of the Education Act 1944 to clarify the groups which have to be taken into account by LEAs in deciding whether free school transport is required in a particular case.

Section 54 enables controlled schools to apply to the Secretary of State for aided status. The governing body of a controlled school, after consultation with the LEA, will have to publish their proposals, enabling objections to be made to the Secretary of State during a two-month period. In considering the proposals, the Secretary of State will have to be satisfied that the governing body is able and willing to meet the financial liabilities arising from aided status and to pay the LEA any compensation for capital expenditure at the school.

Section 55 enables the Secretary of State to decide the amount of compensation to be paid to the LEA under Section 54 if the governing body and the authority fail to agree a figure.

Section 56 requires a school or college governing body to make such reports and returns to the Secretary to State and to provide any other information as he may need for the exercise of his functions.

Section 57 lays a new duty on LEAs to provide, free of charge, appropriate information and training for school governors.

Section 58 establishes a new framework of the payment of travelling and subsistence allowances by LEAs to school and college governors.

Section 59 repeals the provision in Section 4 of the Education Act 1944 for two central advisory councils for education.

Section 60 repeals the provision in Section 5 of the Education Act 1944 which requires the Secretary of State to make an annual report to Parliament.

Section 61 provides that no one aged under 18 may serve as a governor of a further education college unless he or she is a student of the institution.

Section 62 enables the Secretary of State to make regulations to extend the public's right to access to the papers of school and college governing bodies.

Part V Supplemental

Sections 63–67 contain supplemental provisions concerning the making of orders and regulations (Section 63), expenses (Section 64), interpretation (Section 65), commencement (Section 66), and short title (Section 67).

Schedules 1–6 deal respectively with grouped schools; new schools; appeals against exclusion on discipline groups; consequential amendments to other legislation; transitional and savings provisions; and repeals.

[From *DES News*, November 1986 pp 146–153]

CURRICULUM 11–16: HMI PAPERS: SCHOOLS AND SOCIETY; THE WORLD OF WORK

Section Two of the HMI 11–16 working papers of 1977 considered the relationship between schools and society and dealt with questions of political expectations, the general accountability of schools to society, the place of technology, leisure and citizenship and the importance of expressed values:

'Education' and 'Society' are elusive concepts. The terms are used easily enough in casual conversation, but their precise definition is a difficult and continuing exercise, not least because the concepts change over time. Another difficulty is that education has two distinct and yet interdependent roles in relation to society. First, the educational system is charged by society – in the sense of parliamentary will – with equipping young people to take their place as citizens and workers in adult life, and to begin to form attitudes to the prevailing patterns in standards and behaviour. In so doing they will immediately encounter assumptions concerning the nature of accepted norms, and the desirability or otherwise of given social and economic arrangements. Secondly there is the responsibility for educating the 'autonomous citizen', a person able to think and act for herself or himself, to resist exploitation, to innovate and to be vigilant in the defence of liberty. These two functions do not always fit easily together.

Nevertheless both functions are necessary, each acting upon the other. We all belong to groups of some kind, everyone depends upon other people for survival in a complex, technology-based economy which itself is part of a complex international economy. At the same time we are aware of being individual, and there is a necessary tension between obligations and rights. As well as 'socialising' the young by making them aware of their obligations and behavioural responsibilities as members of society, schools have also to teach them about their rights and qualities as individuals.

An insufficient analysis of society will tend to ignore or play down the function of the groups to which we all belong: the family, the peer group, the club, the union, the party, the interest group and so on. The concept of the 'social organism' so prevalent and influential leaves out a good deal more. Any society is based, though not exclusively, upon an economic system, and one requirement of educating pupils to take a place in society is to inform them of how to live and work in such an economy. A society is held together by certain common beliefs and patterns of behaviour, even if and when these are under attack or changing quite rapidly, and any society has a given set of political arrangements, an apparatus of state and authority. We must be clear about the nature and purposes of the 'socialisation' element of education before the more precise obligations of schools can be examined. Any educational discussion quickly reminds us of the compelling special pleas that can and must be made on behalf of minorities. Religious and ethnic minorities are the ones more commonly quoted, but there are many others, for example, the handicapped (itself a rather vague concept), those compelled to move about the country, and children from broken homes whose experience of 'family' is often a wide and unhappy deviation from the norm.

The plurality of such interests and groups in society should be seen as a possible strength. There are many areas of common ground occupied by minorities, for example an interest in toleration and concern for others, in order, in a strong and healthy economy. Schools can obviously do a great deal to make these things plain, and to encourage behaviour appropriate to these ends.

There are also groups of a different kind, who see society as it is at present constituted as oppressive and objectionable. It is very unlikely that the mass of citizens in general, or that parents and local education authorities in particular, would countenance a curriculum for violent change, still less that they would be willing to pay for it. For the purposes of curriculum planning we need to have in mind the 'virtuous citizen', probably living as part of a family, in a largely urban, technology-based industrial society, with minority cultures, working in general towards a social harmony which can accommodate change and differences. It is in relation to some such requirements that the school's role has to be considered.

It is clear that schools have multiple obligations and purposes. They service both society and the individual. They are part of a complex system by which a country aims to sustain and improve its position in the world, but schools are also places – though of course not the only places – where pupils should be helped to develop to the full their individual talents and interests irrespective of whether these can be put to immediate practical use. Hence schools must concern themselves both with preparing adolescents for the adult world, and with helping them to achieve growth, confidence and independence.

The curriculum, the expression of this compromise, is the public expression of the school's educational thinking. It is no new idea to speak of it as a treaty between school and community; it must be continuously reviewed and renegotiated in the light of the differences between the changing demands and expectations of society and the current educational philosophies in our schools. Neither society nor the schools should be the sole arbiter of what is taught and learned.

In the absence of any central control over education in this country, the continuous review and renegotiation of the curriculum is not a simple matter. Major curriculum changes can result only from agreement among a number of different parties, including local authorities, schools, examination boards, and higher and further education. None of these parties specifically represents the interest of the amorphous body which we call society, but all of them are sensitive to the expectations of society as voiced both by consumers of education – the employers, in the widest sense – and by the general public particularly parents, politicians and the media. One of the major difficulties lies in establishing procedures to discover or foster a consensus among the different interested parties as to what schools can reasonably be expected to achieve.

As schools try to reflect or to react to the multiple expectations of society, society for its part must try to define its priorities more clearly. It does not speak with one voice. In a world of pluralist values the messages received by schools can be contradictory and confusing. The acquisitive urge and the sense of social service exist side by side. Industry asks for a conformist work discipline from some but for initiative and a competitive spirit from others. Value systems are changing rapidly and attitudes towards such problems as violence, sexual morality, and the boundaries of tolerance are increasingly unclear. There are obvious contradictions in a society which implicitly or explicitly advocates materialism and moral laissez-faire but expects the young to be responsible. The role of women continues to change and with it, inevitably, the role of men. Both contribute to the care and upbringing of children. There are expectations that the school should contribute to the development of an understanding of the needs of children within a great variety of social backgrounds. In defining its expectations of schools, society must be careful to match these with its actual needs. For instance, expectations are usually, indeed only too often, expressed in terms of examination results (school leavers are expected to have achieved certain grades at O–level or in CSE examinations), whereas in practice the demands of the job are usually very different. Examination results may offer some evidence of a genuine application to work; they do not necessarily say much about other desirable qualities, such as initiative, the capacity to solve problems, or the ability to get on with other people.

Society tends to expect a finished product from schools, whereas it appears to need young people who have acquired certain essential skills, who have learned to work on their own, who have been encouraged to think for themselves and to discriminate, and whose earlier education will enable them to benefit from further education and training.

This is as true of the education of girls as of boys. At one time society may demand that attention must be given to the role of the individual within the family, to the preparation of pupils for parenthood; at another time, society will allege that such preparation is not a job for the school and that obtaining good examination results in traditional and acceptable subjects should take precedence. The ambivalence of society's attitudes has long been epitomised in its approach to girls' education. But women have taken their place alongside men in working life. This country is committed to equal opportunity in education, which must lead to some redistribution of responsibilities within the home, as well as in the world of work.

Social objectives

Social objectives do not require the introduction of new subjects into the curriculum. Most of the necessary knowledge can be transmitted through established subjects or combinations of them. Every subject offers opportunities of encouraging the skills and attitudes needed – skills of independent study, of communication and discussion, of cooperation, and of discrimination. Everything that goes on in a school, in and out of the classroom, can contribute to social objectives or, conversely, can impede their realisation, although some objectives will be best served in the classroom and others through activities outside the school.

But above all, the objectives must be realised through the general ethos of the school, through the nature of the personal relationships in the classroom, through a match between the aims of the school and its organisation and through the daily example of all the adults with whom the pupils are in contact. Attitudes cannot be taught, but teachers who are both caring and challenging, tolerant of error but consistent in setting high standards, and skilful in getting pupils to participate in their learning, will, whatever their specialisms, substantially contribute to all the social objectives that are a proper part of education.

In the realisation of social objectives, much will also depend on the quality of the advice and encouragement that individual pupils are given by members of staff who have a close knowledge of them and enjoy their respect and confidence. Pupils should be helped to understand their individual situations and to develop the personal resources for dealing with them. A precondition of active and purposeful study is the development of a caring atmosphere and of correspondingly good personal relationships. As schools have grown, and organisation has become more complex, the opportunities for teachers to know each pupil will have decreased. Many teachers, in large schools teach two or three hundred pupils a week: in religious education, the problem is often acute. Most schools have found it necessary to set up a pastoral network, but only when all staff feel involved is the academic work effectively supported by this network. No pastoral system can function satisfactorily divorced from the working life of the school.

The third section of the 11–16 working papers was devoted to the part that schools needed to play in the preparation of pupils for work:

The World of Work

There is a danger that the 'world of work', if too narrowly identified, will be seen in isolation from the overall business of living in adult society. To help young people cope with the experience of entering employment is to help them to continue to find their identity as human beings, individuals in society, in larger or smaller groups. For some it will be an enjoyable enlargement of experience: for others it will be a raw, hard and often casual world; all employers are not enlightened, and those who discuss too impatiently schools and their achievements may fail to appreciate what many young people have to offer.

The 16-year-old school leaver should have a foundation that comes from knowing what it is to have done a job well, to have faced up to problems and to have tried to solve them. As we said in Section 2, schools should have developed in their pupils some sense of obligation to other people and sensitivity to their needs and interests, as well as some growing sense of sympathy and understanding with people of a variety of beliefs and practices and cultural backgrounds. All these capacities are most certainly going to be put to the test. In addition, the 16-year-old should have the beginning of a real idea of what paid employment means, of its complexities, duties and rights, and of the uncertainties and fluctuations that some or many will have to face for much and in some cases all of their active life. To receive a pay packet, to work out the deductions, and to face the cost of living can appear to have nothing to do with what one did at school. The links must be made to be real and explicit.

The world of work is extensive as well as complex; it includes any context in which people try to earn their living. It is important that the term 'worker' is not narrowly defined to refer only to those people who man an assembly line. Not all workers in this country are employed by large corporations – the small firms and the self-employed are not only important but of much importance in many parts of the country. Manufacturing is by no means the largest sector of industry and what has often been called 'white-collar work' is increasing. The flexibility that employment will demand in the future makes it important for young people to be adaptable and ready to accept retraining. A substantial number still receives no systematic education after the age of 16, but it is becoming more common for school leavers to find jobs where training and further education are expected and looked forward to. The specific requirements of particular forms of employment will vary greatly; all pupils nevertheless will need a range of general skills, appropriate attitudes and some real, hard knowledge about this world of work.

When a school has considered carefully the general demands which the working life makes, it should accept the responsibility to organise its curriculum to equip its leavers with competence in appropriate skills. During this process a school will have to clarify what it expects pupils to be able to do at the age of 16.

There would probably be wide agreement that most pupils should:

(i) be able to participate effectively in a conversation; set down clearly what they want to express; write letters and simple descriptive reports

(ii) be at ease with diagrams, symbols and graphs; have competence in arithmetic; understand money and the common units of measurement; use a pocket calculator

(iii) possess the dexterity and physical control necessary to develop manipulative skills

(iv) be able to draw on and apply the skills required to tackle a problem scientifically

(v) have developed capacity for reasoning and judgement.

In all these aspects there is need to consider the levels of competence that are appropriate and attainable for individual pupils, and the implications for teaching methods.

Skills can be taught without the introduction of a narrow or specialised vocational training. Every subject to be found in the curriculum of a school can and should make some contribution, but if transfer of skills is to occur then the scope for transfer must be made explicit to the pupils. This requires close cooperation between subject departments within a school as well as attention to the application of specific skills in the outside world.

Pupils' attitudes

The development of a sense of values and of responsible attitudes towards work itself and towards individuals with whom they deal are as important to young employees as the development of skills.

It is essential that pupils have experience at school of what it is to work individually and in groups, to work sometimes independently and sometimes under supervision. Many attitudes traditionally valued by schools, such as the appreciation of quality, a pride in work, a concern for accuracy, a willingness to cooperate, to take responsibility, and to sustain the effect needed to complete a task are equally relevant to the world of work. The links must be self-evident. Similarly schools can educate pupils to value punctuality and neatness, and to be sensitive to safety requirements.

Every department ought to be aware of the ways in which it can make a contribution to the formation of positive attitudes, for this does not happen automatically. So often attitudes are formed unconsciously. Pupils are influenced by the atmosphere of a place, by what is not done and what is left unsaid, by the interaction that they have with staff and the other adults they meet. Personalities play an important part in the transmission of values and pupils meet their teachers as people, not just as instructors.

INDEX

The following abbreviations are used in this index:

DES – Department of Education and Science
HMI – Her Majesty's Inspectorate
LEA – Local Education Authority